Andrea,

Make it happen!

My Big Asset
Home Buying Simplified

by
Brett Roessel

Results Press
Unit 229
#180, 8601 Lincoln Blvd.
Los Angeles, California
90045

www.theresultspress.com

ISBN: 978-1-953089-00-7

First Edition

Copyright©2020 by Brett Roessel

FOREWORD

Each generation asserts they face greater complexities than the previous in fulfilling their dream of homeownership. While one can argue the veracity of that claim one constant remains paramount through generations and that is the immeasurable value of sound advice and counsel home buyers require. The great irony we face along the path towards home ownership is this - what should be an exciting and exhilarating experience often leaves home buyers feeling overwhelmed and quite stressed through the transaction. This can be substantially mitigated if guided by an experienced professional. This brings us to the author of this insightful book, Brett Roessel.

Brett's 20+ plus years of successful experience in the financial sector are made quite evident in this book. He has put forth an excellent body of work that will undoubtedly catapult homeowners up the learning curve in manner that is easy to understand and ingest towards deeper comprehension of home financing needs.

Home ownership is the dream of most. It should not be riddled with angst and confusion. This book cuts through all that and serves as an effective tool for those looking to silence the white noise of what is seemingly a complex experience.

Albert Collu

TABLE OF CONTENTS

CHAPTER ONE
FINANCIAL LITERACY

"The number one problem in today's generation and economy is the lack of financial literacy."

~ Alan Greenspan

When I started my career in banking over 20 years ago, my reasons were very different than why I am still in financial services today. I was 18 years old and I worked as a summer student at a major financial institution. From there, I started working full-time as a customer services representative and then moved into processing. Eventually, I started working with clients as a mortgage adviser and have spent the rest of my career in this position.

The reason I started in this industry was because I wanted a job. As a summer student, that's exactly what I got. The reason I stayed goes much deeper. I am sure you can appreciate that a person doesn't continue in an industry for 20+ years just because it's a job. A few might, but certainly not me.

I fell in love with teaching people about how money works. I was on the front lines as a teller, looking people in the eye as I helped them deposit their paycheques and pay their bills. I was the one who updated their bank books and prepared their travelers' cheques for their vacations. Credit cards were not very accessible back in those days. I was in a position to see people at their best and at their worst.

I was privy to watch the balances of many client accounts and I started to realize firsthand how many people were actually living paycheque to paycheque. Eventually, I moved into my role as a Financial Advisor. This was Cloud-Nine for me. I was so excited to get this position. It meant so much more to me than just a pay raise. That was nice, of course, but I mostly enjoyed the fulfillment I received from sitting kneecap to kneecap with clients who were about to make the single biggest purchase of their lifetime—buying their home.

The more I met with clients, the happier I was. It also worried me. Over the many years and thousands of mortgages I have completed, it didn't take me long to realize most people really don't know that much about how money works. Here I was, I young man in my mid-20's, financing mortgages for $250K+, $400K+ or $1MM+ for gainfully-employed adults who didn't know how the mortgage actually worked. I found out it went much deeper than that. Most of them didn't know how money worked. That's why I am so proud to have the career I now have. I am in a position to help people learn about how money works, and more importantly, how to make money work for them.

I had worked at the same bank for my entire career, up until four years ago when I left to become an independent broker. I had an amicable departure and am forever grateful for the friends and colleagues I have from working at this major financial institution. I also have tremendous gratitude for all the training and mentorship I received. The fact is, I wanted more. I wanted to *be* more. I wanted to *give* more.

That's why I went into business for myself. I know I can help a lot more people mortgage their Big Asset if I was working outside the confines of a conventional financial institution. Now I have access to funding sources to which I didn't have access before. I am not limited by the products I can offer, the advice I can give or the strategies I can implement.

Here we are now--The reason I wrote this book. I am only one person and I can only physically meet with so many people from day-to-day.

However, I know there are ways to reach more people who need the information contained in these pages. Through information in these pages, I can reach far more people with whom I could possibly sit down and meet in person. On the other hand, if the content of this book gets through to even one person and they can change the course of their life, it will be worth it.

Another part of my story is I was raised in a low-income neighborhood and the youngest of five children. I was heavily involved in year-round sports, as were all my brothers (I have two) and sisters (also two). Keeping all of us involved in sports was expensive for two parents of modest means. That meant paying for registration x5, equipment x5 and all the travel x5. All this, in addition to working to provide for the family and parenting all five children. My parents are amazing. They taught me a lot about hard work, honesty, loyalty, and life in general. But the one thing they weren't able to teach me was how money works.

Most people think they know how money works. They go to work and get a pay cheque. The money goes into their account and they spend it. For the most part, that's about the limit of our financial literacy. It's also these same people who gripe about the statement, *'It takes money to make money.'* They're certainly not wrong. The part they are missing is a person doesn't already have to be wealthy to make money. The second part they never talk about is it doesn't matter how much money you have. It only matters what you do with the money you have.

I am really worried. The problem of financial illiteracy is getting worse, not better. FINRA conducted a 2015 study about the current state of financial literacy[i]. Study participants were asked five questions covering aspects of economics and finance encountered in everyday life, such as compound interest, inflation, principles relating to risk and diversification, the relationship between bond prices and interest rates and the impact a shorter term can have on total interest payments over the life of a mortgage. 63% of the respondents had three or fewer correct answers. That figure is up from 58% in 2009.

They also observed that 58% of respondents did not compare offers from different companies when shopping for credit cards, suggesting a gap in applying financial decision-making skills to real life situations. The end results are higher interest rates and consequently, higher borrowing costs.

It's not surprising, is it? Report after report suggest most people are on pace to retire broke. The Globe and Mail recently reported, "A large percentage of older, working Canadians are heading into retirement without adequate savings to keep them out of poverty"[ii]. This came on the heels of a report published by pension consultant Richard Shillington. In other words, the numbers look something like this:

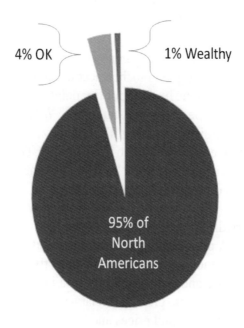

95% of people in North America are on pace to live at or below the poverty line. In other words--broke. 4% will be Okay, which means they can afford to live the same lifestyle they are living now. 1% will retire wealthy. That is the status of financial literacy as we know it today. It's not being taught in our schools and it's not being taught by the institutions. Before we jump into the detail of your Big Asset and the value of home ownership, I need to make sure you understand a few key concepts first. If you already know these concepts, congratulations! You are better off than most people you know. I encourage you to refresh your memory. If you have never heard these concepts before, make sure you pay special attention. This may just be the thing you need to set you up for life.

Cash Flow Pie

Cash flow, in its simplest form, is the difference between the how much you make and how much you spend. I like to keep things simple.

$$\text{Cash Flow} = \frac{\text{Money In}}{\text{Every Month}} - \frac{\text{Money Out}}{\text{Every Month}}$$

OBJ

The simple math here is when you have more money coming in every month than you do going out, your cash flow is positive. Less money coming in than going out is negative cash flow. That means there are ONLY three ways to increase cash flow (or capital):

A. Increase your income.
B. Decrease your expenses.
C. Both A & B

It really is that simple.

The Cash Flow Pie describes how the average monthly budget is allocated within a typical household. When you split up the monthly cash flow of a typical household, approximately half is spent on living expenses. This includes food, clothing, mortgage/rent, utilities, entertainment, recreation and other daily living items. A significant portion of the cash flow is spent on debt, included credit cards, car loans and personal loans. Another substantial portion of the cash flow is used to pay taxes--most notably, income tax and sales tax. There is a small part of this cash flow which goes towards savings. However, this portion is usually very small and subjective. Most people spend their income first and save what's left. Sometimes they have more month than money and the first thing which stops is contributing to the savings.

When this typical family wants to increase their savings, the first place they look to cut is their lifestyle from their living expenses. They create something called a *budget* and put unreasonable expectations about how they need to live from month-to-month. A budget is another word for a financial diet, and we all know how diets don't work.

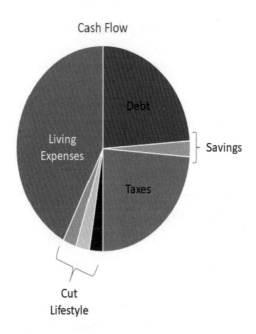

What if we increased the financial literacy of our friends and family?

What if we showed them ways to reduce the amount of interest they pay on their debt or different ways to save on taxes? How much of a difference would that make in their lives? If that's where we started, they would be far more likely to succeed as opposed to cutting out all the things they enjoy and go to work every day to afford.

That is what My Big Asset is here to do. Deliver the financial education people need to make better decisions for themselves. And we start with their biggest purchase--mortgaging their home. More is coming!

Rule of 72

Are you familiar with the Rule of 72? It's a brilliant calculation invented by Einstein in which explains how to calculate the value of compound interest. You can certainly go to University and learn how to use the formula to calculate the future value of a series of cash flows. I believe they teach it in third year Finance. Or, you can just take the next few minutes and read a little about this freakishly accurate rule.

The rule is: Divide the interest rate by 72 and that will give you the number of years it takes for your money to double.

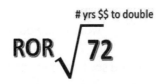

$$\text{ROR} \sqrt{\overset{\text{\# yrs \$\$ to double}}{72}}$$

For example. Suppose that the average savings rate your bank offers is 2%. That is super generous, I know. I believe the average savings account rate as of the writing of this book is much lower. I like simple and this number keeps the math simple. Divide the 2% by 72 and it will take 36 years for that money to double. In other words, if you put $10,000 into a savings account compounding at 2%, it will take 36 years to grow to $20,000. Simple, right? That's one of the many reasons why Einstein was such a genius.

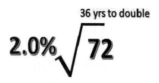

Compound interest doesn't discriminate. It works the same for debt as it does for our savings. Let's assume the average credit card rate is 18%. This might not be exact, but it is close to a reasonable average. Not to mention, it makes the math simple and I already mentioned how I like to keep it simple. Divide 18% by 72 and it will take four years for your debt to double. In other words, a credit card balance of $10,000 will double to $20,000 in only four years!

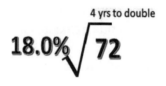

Is it any wonder why the cash flow pie looks the way it does? People are struggling to grow their savings which only doubles every 36 years, but their debt doubles every four years. This isn't a have-not problem. This is an education problem. Can you see how important this information is for people to know? On the flipside, if debt doubles every four years, do you think it's pretty important to know how the banks work? Yes, or yes? Well, that's the bag of money. Don't put this book down yet and continue reading.

Bag of Money

The bag of money is a super simple explanation of what happens to your money once it gets into your account. When you deposit your hard-earned income into your bank account, the bank takes your money and invests those funds with a professional money manager. Those money managers invest the money for the bank, take their fees (around 3-5%) and then provide the bank with a net return between 12-15%. Since you have put your money on deposit with the bank, they take part of their return and provide you with 1-3% for the opportunity to rent your money.

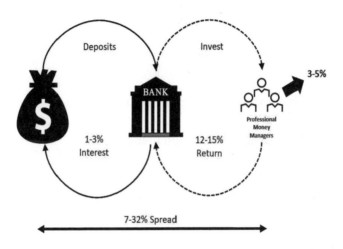

I admit this may be a little oversimplified and there is much more to this system, if you're willing to admit this is valuable information to know. The question is how to find ways to bypass the bank and get access to the same money managers. That may need a completely different book!

Just by knowing these three concepts, you are already ahead of 80% of the rest of North America. Do you find that surprising? You might be thinking, *"All of this information is great, Brett, but it still takes money to make money, right?"* Well, you're partly right. It's more important what you do with the money you have.

© Randy Glasbergen / glasbergen.com

"I have a diversified retirement plan:
sometimes I wish for money, sometimes
I hope for money, sometimes I pray for money..."

There are two things you need make sure you understand…

It's not about how much money you make:

- It's about how much money you keep.
- It's also what you do with the money you have.

How Much You Keep

Here is why the amount of money you keep is more important than the amount of money you make--you only have discretion over the money you keep! Let me put this another way. Would you rather make $100,000 and keep $60,000 of it or make $80,000 and keep $70,000? It's not a trick question. The short answer is keeping the $70,000. Of course, there are hundreds of conditions which affect how much money you keep, but do you think with a little education, you might be in a better position to keep more of what you make?

> **Learning Lesson**
>
> Pay yourself first is a strategy spoken about by many money experts and independently wealthy investors. One of the better known explanations was written by David Chilton, author of The Wealthy Barber.
>
> Chilton writes that to be wealthy, a person should take the first 10% of their net income and deposit into an investment account. The remainder should be used to pay bills, living expenses and debts. As income grows, so will the 10%.
>
> Saving is a habit and can be difficult for many to develop it. If 10% is not attainable, any % of net income will do. What IS important is to develop the habit of paying yourself first.

When you think back to the Cash Flow Pie earlier in this chapter, the whole pie represents the amount you make while the savings sliver represents how much of it you get to keep. You can really bust your butt to try and grow the size of that pie by begging your boss for a raise or working a second or even third job to earn extra income. Or you can rearrange the slices within the pie to increase how much you get to keep. The difference is a little financial education.

What You Do with What You Have

Regardless if you are able to keep more or less of the amount you make, the second key is what you do with the money you have. Even if all you did was increase your savings rate by 1-2%, your doubling periods would change dramatically. That's the power of compound interest. You can either make compounding work for you or you can permit the financial services institutions to use it against you.

I am making it my personal mission to get this information out to as many people as possible. The amount of money most people are leaving on the table because they don't understand how mortgages work or which solutions are right for them is outrageous. There are a ton of misunderstandings about the true cost of borrowing. I am not talking about a few pennies here and there. The amount of money leaking out of homeowners' pockets is in the tens of thousands for most mortgage holders.

My only goal here is to put people in a position for them to make better decisions about their financial well-being. There are a ton of financial instruments for which we all need some education. Credit is one of those instruments which is widely misunderstood and yet has a significant impact on our financial lives. Your credit is your financial reputation for the rest of your life. Much more on that coming in later chapters.

Our focus for the rest of this book is going to be on the single biggest purchase most people will ever make--their home. The content I am going to share is going to change the game for:

- First-Time Home Buyers
- Mortgage Refinance
- Repeat mortgage clients
- Renters
- The families of the people in each of these groups

I am excited to share this journey with you.

Before we go too deep into the rest of this book, we need to discuss how most people buy their homes. There are few people who have enough cash flow to buy a home paid-in-full. If you have learned anything about the time value of money from the Rule of 72, you have probably already figured out that paying cash for a home may not even be the best financial decision.

If most people are either unable to buy their home paid-in-full, or at least decide not to, what do they do?

That's when the mortgage comes into play.

The modern mortgage actually has its roots going back to the 12th century. The mortgage concept dates as far back as 2000 B.C. in Mesopotamia[iii]. Simply put, a mortgage is a contract or agreement to lend money for the purchase of a property in which the buyer agrees to pay back the principal plus a sum of interest and where the lender takes security in the title of the property until the debt and interest is fully repaid.

mort·gage
/ˈmôrgij/ ◄)

noun

1. a legal agreement by which a bank or other creditor lends money at interest in exchange for taking title of the debtor's property, with the condition that the conveyance of title becomes void upon the payment of the debt.

Here are some terms you need to know:

Purchase Price	The price negotiated for the price of your home.
Mortgage Agreement	The binding agreement between lender and borrower.
Mortgage Amount	The total principal amount borrowed.
Down Payment	Cash down payment applied towards the purchase price of the home.
Mortgage Interest Rate	The borrowing rate used to calculate the interest charges on the mortgage amount.
Mortgage Payment	The total payment required every period.
Payment Frequency	The number of times per year the mortgage payment is required.
Compound Interest	Interest paid on interest.
Compounding Periods	The number of times per year the interest is compounded.

*Please refer to the glossary for a complete list of terms.

You have just received a crash course in financial literacy which not even University students are being taught. Armed with this knowledge, you are well on your way to changing the financial legacy for you and your entire family.

But that's not all. Are you ready for more?

o   Only 1% of North Americans are expected to retire wealthy, while 95% are on pace to retire at or below the poverty line.

o   The cash flow pie is split between living expenses, taxes, debt, and a small sliver of savings.

o   The rule of 72 calculates compounding and how many years it takes for your money to double.

o   Banks will take your money, invest it with professional money managers and keep most of the return.

o   It's not how much you make it's how much you keep.

o   The first mortgages were recorded going back to 2000 B.C.

CHAPTER TWO
THE POWER OF HOME OWNERSHIP

*"Owning a home is a keystone of wealth—
both financial affluence and emotional security."*

~ Suze Orman

There is a point when a house becomes a home. I'm sure you know what I mean. I recognize it simply by listening to how people speak about where they live. They say things like, "I love my home," or, "I can't wait to get home." I have never heard someone say, "I love my house." It even sounds weird to say out loud.

Why does it sound strange? Because it doesn't happen.

There is so much more to owning a home compared to living in a house, condo, or apartment. We *live* in all of them. We sleep in these places, cook our meals, socialize, and take care of our families in these places. We also do many of these activities at a hotel when we travel, but none would say that's a home. So, what is it that makes a house MORE than just a place where we live?

Suze Orman sums it up perfectly. Home ownership forms a keystone of affluence and security in our life. For many of you reading this, you may be thinking to yourself, "Well yeah, of course." Owning a home is not an option for many people throughout the world, especially for those outside of North America. There are financial limitations, risk limitations, government interventions, access to land and many other reasons which prevent people from owning their homes.

We are fortunate in North America that home ownership rates are greater than 60% on average.[iv] The worldwide statistics are a little sparse because many of the countries with the biggest populations have poor systems for this kind of data. However, I feel it is safe to suggest that home ownership among the world's seven-billion people is fairly low overall.

The power of home ownership is a source of accomplishment. Buying a home is something few people around the world get to experience. I was fortunate enough to travel the world at a young age and witnessed lots of poverty firsthand. That was when I realized why people immigrate to Canada and why one of their proudest accomplishments is buying a home.

When newcomers to Canada buy a home, it feels as if they won the lottery. They have a sense of:

o   I do own this home.
o   This lawn in mine.
o   These four walls and this roof are mine.

That sense of pride compels them to tell everyone they know about being homeowners. That is one of the reasons why I love helping people new to Canada and first-time homebuyers purchase their first home. I experience an amazing feeling being the one who helps them live out their dreams. There can only be one first.

I think you can see where I am going with this. The power of home ownership reaches much deeper than the foundation (see what I did there?) and well beyond simply providing shelter.

You may have heard of this scientist named Maslow or about his Hierarchy of Needs. Without getting too academic, Maslow developed a hierarchy to explain how people are motivated, starting at the bottom with *physiological needs*. Once those needs are met, their motivation then comes from the next level up and so on until they reach self-actualization[v].

Here is why I wanted you to know this. The first level is *physiological needs*. This includes SHELTER. The next level is *safety needs* which includes PERSONAL SECURITY and PROPERTY. Once *safety needs* are fulfilled, people may then begin to be motivated by love and belonging. These needs include FAMILY and SENSE OF CONNECTION. Then *esteem* manifests, including STATUS and RECOGNITION. Lastly, a person is motivated by *self-actualization* once all other needs are met. *Self actualization* occurs when a person pursues their need for FULFILLMENT.

The power of home ownership satisfies, at least in part, each of the basic needs which motivates a person! We don't need a four-year college degree to understand what Maslow is talking about, especially when it comes to home ownership.

In my experience of helping thousands of clients over my 20+ year career, I've witnessed by the looks on their faces when they purchase their homes that the power of home ownership satisfies these needs. I know many clients become frustrated with the process when the time draws near to closing. They're excited to take possession and move into their new home but still have to deal with legal matters, dotting I's and crossing T's. After the transactional parts are completed, a huge sense of relief washes over them and they move into the transformational process.

They start to visualize how they are going to arrange the furniture--where they will put the sofa, which room will the kids take or where will they put the tables. They experience a legitimate feeling of pride and say to themselves, "I am a very proud homeowner of this particular home."

I have never experienced a closing where my client purchased a home because they'd merely settled. None of my clients have ever said, "I'm just going to buy this house because it's the only one available." Every one of my clients has waited for that perfect house (or condo, or apartment) they can call home, the home which satisfies all of their needs (see how smart Maslow is?) and they can picture themselves living in the home for a long time.

Why else would the sellers and buyers of houses become emotional over the same transaction for different reasons? The sellers are leaving memories behind, while the buyers are excited for the memories they are going to make. There is massive pride in ownership.

Pride in Ownership

The feeling of attachment and pride I see people exhibit is not surprising. They put a ton of work into buying their home! Buyers put the work in to saving for a down payment, shop for a home and complete all the paperwork required by lenders, lawyers and governments. Some people have one home for their entire life. They should be proud to own it. Perhaps they raised their family in that home and have left notches on the doorway marking how tall their children were on each birthday. Maybe there is a favorite tree or a swing on a tree branch.

This reminds me of a very funny scene in *Christmas Vacation* starring Chevy Chase. In the movie, Chevy's character (Clark Griswold) spends a whole winter's day on his day off putting up a Christmas display. This is not just any display. This is the best display on the block. After a couple of failed attempts, at the big reveal, when he plugs in the power cord, the display finally lights up and it's glorious! The smile on Clark Griswold's face while he admires his own handywork with his family is priceless.

That is the power of home ownership. There is a measurable pride which comes from owning your home. Sometimes it is enormous, like that of Clark Griswold, while at other times it is more subtle, such as the feeling you get when you walk in the door after a long, hard day and you are *home*.

This makes a lot of sense, doesn't it? You experience satisfaction right from the start of the homebuying process through to taking possession, and many years after living your life in your home. In my 20+ years of working with mortgage clients, every client bought their home because they wanted to.

I can literally see the pride in their faces as clients start the process of shopping for a home, get approved for their mortgage and then take possession. The pride of ownership begins long before the transaction is completed and extends far beyond the completion of the purchase.

Source of Security

The most talked about form of security home ownership brings to people is financial. Security, according our friend Maslow, satisfies our need for safety. There are several other ways that home ownership helps satisfy that need.

1. Financial Security

The financial security of home ownership is the most publicly discussed benefit of buying your home. Your home is an asset which may grow in value. I know you have probably read alternative explanations in the media and publications, but for our purposes, we will keep this simple.

Your home provides financial security by growing in value. The Canadian Real Estate Association (CREA) shows the average growth of Canadian real estate over 13 years going back to 2005[vi]. Take a look at the chart below. The bottom line is the one we're interested in. It represents the average residential price for all properties across Canada. Notice the overall trend? It's upwards. I am not a rocket scientist, but I know that when a trend line goes up from left to right, that means good things for our money.

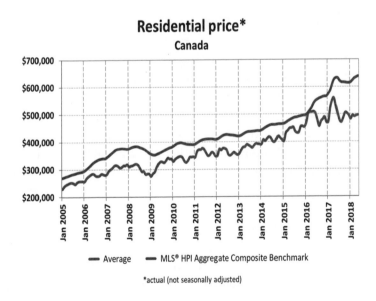

Did you also notice that the left-to-right upward trend is not a straight line? There are a few ups and downs along the way. Although owning your home provides financial security from appreciation and growth, it is not guaranteed.

This is where I need to inform you that these figures are for illustration and discussion only and are not to be interpreted as financial advice. I am not an accountant, lawyer or investment adviser. Any investments taken on carry risk of which you need to be aware.

Back to financial security. If you had purchased your home in 2005 for approximately $230,000, your home could be worth about $500,000 13 years later. That growth provides some level of financial security. There will be more on this in the coming chapters.

2. Have a Home where Owners can Go

Homeowners enjoy another sense of security and safety which others do not. They experience the assurance that they will always have their home where they can go. They know they can never be evicted from where they live. Homeowners do not need to fear the owner of a leased or rented place will never sell the property and force them to move. They have a feeling of security in knowing a landlord will suddenly stop-by for a visit to check up on the place.

People have a real sense of safety and security where they have certainty. I am not suggesting absolute certainty here because that doesn't exist. Just reasonable certainty. Homeowners are the only ones who get to decide when they choose to move.

3. Protecting our Families

Any shelter may reasonably protect our families. However, some are better than others. A tent is better than a lean-to, and a cabin is better than a tent. I can make an argument that a rental house may provide just as much security for your family as a house you own. The doors and windows lock, there may be a gate and a fence. So, what is it about owning a home that provides owners a greater sense of security for their families?

The answer is *choice*.

Homeowners enjoy the privilege of choice which others do not. Homeowners can CHOOSE to increase the security of their homes without interference. They can choose to put in an alarm system, bars on the windows, motion-activated flood lights, security gates and cameras without having to check in with a landlord or property owner. A homeowner can make their home more secure if they choose.

I am not suggesting owners need to transform their homes into Fort Knox to keep their families safe and secure. Nor am I suggesting anyone who does not own their home is at super high risk of having their family hurt. It merely demonstrates my point. Having the CHOICE to make improvements as a homeowner can provide enough comfort to make your family feel safe and secure.

4. Safe Place to Sleep

This part is really an extension of the last section. Having a safe place to sleep and providing security are interconnected. The distinction I wish to get across here is people can BE secure but still not FEEL safe. I admit it's a subtle distinction. Alternatively, you can FEEL safe but not BE secure.

Let me explain it like this:

Security is the overarching umbrella protecting our safety. We can take measures to increase security. But feeling safe is physical and emotional. The TSA security lineup as you enter the airport is a great example. They have implemented measures to ensure the airport and planes are secure, yet it probably doesn't make a person who has a fear of flying feel any safer.

The difference in that safe feeling homeowners enjoy compared to those who do not own their homes is subtle, but it exists. Homeowners are more likely to get to know their neighbors, the people working in their local grocery stores or nearby restaurants. These behaviors, combined with the opportunity of choice, gives homeowners more of sense of a safe place to sleep than those who don't own their homes.

Are you still not convinced about the power of home ownership? The Georgia Tech Center for Economic Development designed and executed a survey in 2016 about the impact benefactors of Habitat for Humanity received[vii]. Here are some of their findings:

- 74% of homeowners are better able to save money since purchasing their Habitat home, and approximately 71% say they're better able to pay bills on time.
- Nearly all homeowners (98%) feel positive about the future, and 79 percent say their feelings about the future have gotten better since moving into their Habitat home.

○ 43% of respondents have started or completed higher education or training programs since becoming a Habitat homeowner, and 58% indicated that other adults living with them started or completed an educational or training program since moving, as well.

If these results indicate anything, it's that the power of home ownership runs much deeper than a simple real estate transaction. Let's move on to why you're really reading this book. What can becoming a home owner really do for *you*?

Now that you have considered the emotional aspects of why people buy and finance their homes, you're ready for some meaty material into which you can really sink your teeth--what being a homeowner can do for you.

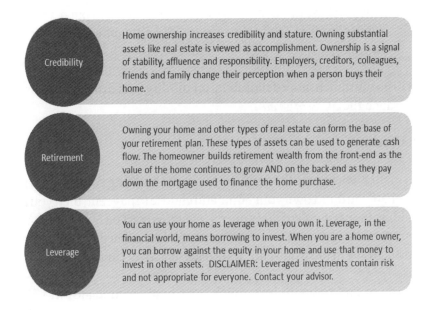

Let's dive a little deeper.

Credibility

Home ownership adds credibility. As I mentioned above, buying large and substantial assets changes how we are perceived by others. This phenomenon is not isolated to buying our homes. It also applies to other luxuries, such as certain types of cars, jewelry, designer clothes and glamorous vacations, to name a few. However, there are a few major differences between this luxury list and purchasing a home when it comes to credibility.

o   The purchase of ANY home increases our credibility regardless of the size of purchase. Employers and creditors consider homeowners more stable and responsible. That doesn't mean this is actually true in all cases because we know it is not.

o   The purchase of a home as a status item also adds to our net worth, while the other items in our luxury list only subtract from our net worth.

I will go into much more detail about credibility later in the book when I introduce the *5C's of Credit.*

Retirement

No matter where you choose to live, you are building somebody's net worth. If you don't own your home and choose to pay rent, then you are building the net worth of the property owner. When you own your home, you are building your personal net worth. As I mentioned above, your net worth grows in the front-end AND back-end over time.

The front-end refers to how much your home appreciates in value. Remember the data earlier in this chapter demonstrating the growth of the average residential price? That is the front-end growth of your home--the difference between the price you paid for your home and the price you can sell it for. Before you get excited about the boost in net worth home ownership will earn you, growth in average real estate prices ranged between 1-5% over the last eight years (Canada)[viii]. To put that in perspective, inflation averages approximately 3%. In short, your buying power will be approximately the same as it is now.

The back-end growth in net worth is earned by paying off the mortgage used to finance the home purchase. This is a benefit exclusively to homeowners. Even if the value of the home grows just a little, paying down the mortgage increases the equity in the home.

Equity = Market Value of the Home - Mortgage Balance on the Home

It should be clear that equity in your home grows by growing market value, reducing the mortgage or both. That equity may then be used as part of a retirement strategy.

Leverage

If you have ever borrowed money to buy something, you're using leverage. You may have used a loan to buy a car or a credit card to buy electronics. Using a mortgage to buy a home is also leverage. The definition of leverage varies depending on the context in which it's discussed. Leverage in this context is using debt to be an appreciating asset.

Leverage may be used when you have equity (see above definition) in your home. You would already have used a mortgage as leverage to buy your home (unless you paid cash). You can also use leverage to borrow against the equity in your home. That money may be used to invest in other assets, such as investment properties, stocks, bonds or any other investment right for you according to your advisor.

The laws and regulations surrounding leverage are very specific. This strategy is not suitable for everyone. Any leveraged strategy should only be carefully considered under advisement from a competent and licensed investment advisor.

Credibility, retirement and leverage are just a few benefits I chose to highlight which homeowners can enjoy. You are a unique individual with unique financial and personal needs. There are as many strategies as there are people, so please make sure that you meet with your mortgage broker or advisor to discuss what's best for you.

In my 20 years of experience as a mortgage broker and advisor, I have seen and heard many stories about what buying a home does for my clients. Every time I sign closing documents with my clients, I observe an overwhelming feeling of accomplishment in them. It doesn't appear to matter if they are first-time homebuyers or are getting into their fifth purchase. The feeling is the same.

The journey for one family with whom I worked is a great example of the emotions of the homebuying journey. I was introduced to a really nice couple. They'd found the single-family detached home they were renting just really wasn't working for their family anymore. The property needed repairs and they were quickly outgrowing the space.

We started their homebuying journey. I was able to get them preapproved on a mortgage with a couple of conditions--they needed to use some of the cash they had saved to pay down some debt and the rest for a down payment. They were beyond excited--so excited they decided to take a family vacation.

The money spent on vacation, combined with a few other financial decisions and changing mortgage rules, meant they no longer qualified for the same terms. Their qualification changed so much that they could no longer shop for the home they needed. Since their son was in a wheelchair, they needed a bungalow with no stairs. None of the homes for which they could now qualify suited their family's needs. They went from excited to overwhelmed.

As time passed, they became stressed about the whole process. That stress triggered a couple of more vacations and other financial decisions which moved them in the opposite direction from buying the home they needed.

The good news is with time, effort, planning and guidance, I was able to get them into their home, one they would love to live in AND which was suitable for their family's needs. Three years after we started, they were finally able to move in and transitioned from being stressed to being excited again, and then finally, fulfilled.

For most people, the decision to make the single biggest purchase of their lifetimes is an enormous commitment. The moment they decide to start the journey is the beginning of an emotional roller coaster.

THE 4 EMOTIONS OF THE HOME-BUYING JOURNEY

The homebuyer's journey starts out very EXCITED. The process for first time homebuyers is new and the thought of what it means to be a homeowner sinks in. All the emotions and reasons we have already discussed in this chapter start flooding in. Repeat homebuyers experience the same emotions about the upcoming change. Their imaginations run wild with all the possibilities for their new homes. For both types of buyers, the excitement of the process is high.

As the journey continues, buyers start to feel OVERWHELMED. They begin to look long and hard at their list of requirements--all of the features they want in their home, such as where they want to buy, how much they want to spend, what size of yard they want, what the kitchen needs to look like and so on. They become overwhelmed as their Realtor puts hundreds of buying options in front of them to review. They buyer becomes overwhelmed by all the paperwork they need to complete as they prepare their mortgage applications and gather all of the documents their mortgage broker is going to need to qualify them for a purchase.

Once buyers cross a little past halfway in the journey, they begin to get STRESSED. They have looked at 20-30 homes and none of them have everything they want. They realize they are going to have to choose which options they may be willing to live without. Their mortgage advisor has now provided them with a preapproval, and it may not be as much as they need. The preapproval may have a number of conditions they didn't expect and could delay their journey. The homebuyer is concerned if their deal is ever going to get done.

Soon the journey ends. The homebuyer has a great team of advisors in their Realtor and Mortgage Broker who have worked their butts off to find the right home and get all the conditions cleared for closing. It is at this point the feeling of FULFILLMENT starts to set in. Purchase offers have been accepted and closing paperwork has been signed. It will only be a matter of weeks now until the buyer can move in.

The feeling of ACCOMPLISHMENT overwhelms the buyer as the funds clear and the home is theirs. They start to make plans to take possession and move into their new home.

That is the power of home ownership.

Savings & Retirement

Can your home be used as part of your savings and retirement plan? The real question here shouldn't be CAN you but rather HOW do you? To answer that question, we need to look back at how planning our savings and retirement has changed over the past 50 years.

When we look back to the 1950's, the prevailing wisdom was people started their career job shortly after finishing high school. People planned to work for that one company for the next 30+ years. They worked hard at their jobs and relied on the company to provide them with raises and promotions to increase their income, hopefully enough to keep pace with inflation and at least maintain the same lifestyle. The goal was to pay off the mortgage as fast as possible and then start saving for retirement.

By the time they were ready to retire, people had paid their home in-full, had acquired a small savings account, had a corporate pension to provide most of their living income in retirement and had a small government pension to supplement. The home was a major cornerstone of the retirement plan because people would have their home to live in and no mortgage to pay off. They could afford to live on the cash flow from a pension and small savings account.

Through the 60's, 70's and 80's, corporations began to shift. They needed more knowledge workers and less laborers. The prevailing strategy shifted to higher education, getting good grades and THEN acquiring a great job at a good company from which you could retire. The retirement plans of that time still used a three-legged stool on which to base their retirement. Owning a home free and clear still formed a cornerstone of the retirement plan because it provided the much-needed place to live which required a minimal cash flow

The economic environment changed considerably through the 90's and into the millennium. Tenure with companies has shortened and people generally have multiple careers in their lifetimes. Combined with corporations reducing their human capital expenses by discontinuing pensions, the three-legged stool quickly lost a leg.

Now, depending on your source, many are concerned that government pensions are dwindling and offer very little support to retirees. That is, of course, if there is any income pool from which to draw in the next 30 years. Our three-legged stool is now down to the one leg--personal savings. Your home is still a cornerstone of your savings and retirement plans, though it may play a more significant part of the plan today.

As a result of life changes, simply paying off the mortgage of your house is not sufficient in a one-legged stool. There simply is not enough time to use strategies which worked in the past. Owning a home is still a cornerstone or a solid savings and retirement plan but it has to be used differently.

There are many who prefer the tangibility of owning a home to store their capital as opposed to buying paper assets such as stocks or bonds. They feel far more empowered by mortgaging a home. There is one problem. You are potentially sitting on a bucket of cash logged up in the walls of your home which you can't access. You can't exactly break off a doorknob and take it to the grocery store to buy a loaf of bread. Thus, paying off your home shouldn't be the only strategy in your retirement plan. Rather, it is one of the cornerstones.

The issue I have seen over and over in my 20+ years in the mortgage industry is that the problem isn't strategy. The problem facing most people is education. Many just don't understand the ins and outs of their financial options, especially when it comes to mortgages.

Here are just a few alternatives of how owning your home can be one of the cornerstones in your retirement plan.

Strategy	Description	Pros	Cons
Paid in Full	Pay off your mortgage in full and then use your mortgage payments towards your savings plan.	• Focused financial strategy. • Minimize the total interest expense paid.	• Lose tons of valuable time to invest. • Need to rely on alternative investments for a source of income in retirement.
Sell the Home	Sell your home in retirement and use the lump sum cash to finance your lifestyle in retirement.	• Converts a free and clear home into cash that can be used in retirement.	• Still need a place to live in retirement and will either need to buy a smaller home or pay rent. • Proceeds may not be enough to finance full retirement fund.
Leverage the Equity	Use the equity in the home to generate cash flow through reverse mortgage or other leverage strategies.	• Ability to create cash flow from a home that is free and clear. • Have a place to live in retirement	• Lose tons of valuable time to invest.
Invest as You Go	Structure your mortgage with interest only payments and invest the principal portion of the payment.	• Take advantage of early investing and the time value of money. • Left with a substantial retirement fund AND a paid off home.	• Leveraged strategies are not right for everyone. • Carries risk and requires savings discipline.

These are just a few strategies with which a mortgage professional can help. The question answered here is how do you use your home as part of your savings and retirement strategy? The strategy which works for you will be different than one which works for someone else. The point here is there is a strategy and all you need is education to discover it.

Use of Equity - Leveraging

One particular couple I worked with in 2015 realized they were not on track for their retirement goals and needed to collapse time frames. This particular couple followed the path they were brought up to believe would get them there. They implemented the only strategy they knew at the time, which was to buy a home and pay it off as quickly as they could. Does that sound familiar?

When I started working with them, they had paid off their home free-and-clear and still were not on track to a livable retirement. How did that happen? It happened because no one gave them the knowledge that there was another way. We helped them to use their home as leverage. They mortgaged $200,000 on their $350,000 home. My client then used the $200,000 as an investment to jumpstart their savings program. The payment on their mortgage was $300 accelerated weekly, which averaged to approximately $1300 per month.

This was where this case got interesting. What do you think will grow faster? Investing $1300 per month every month for 10 years or $200,000 today over 10 years, assuming the growth rate is 5%? If you said the $200,000 will grow faster, then you're right. And not by a little. By a lot!

$1300/month @5% compounded monthly over 120 months (10 years) = $202K
$200,000 @5% compounded monthly over 120 months (10 years) = $329K

Since they are making principle + interest payments as they go, their home will be paid off AND they will have a lump sum of cash to use in retirement. The investment is handled by their trusted investment advisor, so this really is a team effort. Are you starting to see what the power of home ownership can do for people?

I have provided a very simple illustrative example of what we did for this couple. This is what being a homeowner can do for you:

Suppose your home has been appraised at a $500,000 market value and your mortgage balance is $200,000, which will be paid off in the next 10 years. The total equity in your home is $300,000. A leveraged strategy would use some of the equity to buy an investment which we hope to grow over the next 10 years. You decide to use $100,000 and invest in a portfolio recommended by your trusted advisor, for which you expect to earn an annual return of 5%.

Value of Home	$500,000
Balance of Mortgage	$300,000 over 10 Years
Total Equity Available	$200,000
Leveraged Investment	$100,000
Annual Growth Rate	5%
In 10 years....	Paid off House + $64,700

If everything goes according plan over the next 10 years, you will have...
- o   A home paid off free-and-clear

o   An investment return worth $64,700

That is how leveraging works. Homeowners can use this strategy while they are paying down their mortgage or after it is paid-in-full provided, they qualify.

Ideas to Remember

o   Home ownership forms a keystone of affluence and security in our lives.

o   Owning a home brings a sense of pride, security and accomplishment.

o   Credibility, savings/retirement and leverage are just a few benefits afforded to homeowners.

o   Equity = Market Value of the Home - Mortgage Balance on the Home.

o   Four Emotions of the Home-Buying Journey: Excited, Overwhelmed, Stressed, Fulfilled.

o   Owning a home is one cornerstone of a retirement plan but not the only one.

o   Changing times require a look at different strategies when planning for retirement. The old strategies are no longer sufficient or effective.

o   Home equity can be used to build wealth before, during and after the mortgage is paid.

CHAPTER THREE
OWNING VERSUS RENTING

"The single biggest difference between financial success and financial failure is how well you manage your money. It's simple: to master money, you must manage money."

~ *T. Harv Eker*

It is no big secret that we are not given a comprehensive education in how money works. I think that message is pretty clear from Chapter One. That's why I love this quote from T. Harv Eker. He doesn't say, "You need money to make money," or, "Wealth is reserved for a precious few." Financial success comes with how well you manage your money. From my perspective, all this requires is a little bit of education.

I started working with one particular client who had always rented. He decided to buy a home together with a friend of his (who also rented). They felt if they were going to pay toward their landlord's mortgage, they may as well buy and take what they would pay in rent and contribute to pay down their own mortgage. These clients decided to access their RRSP's (Registered Retirement Savings Plans) as part of the first-time homebuyer's plan (discussed in Chapter Four) to provide their required 5% down payment. Their plan was to review their living situation in five years and decide what changes, if any, needed to be made. As it turned out, they'd both found themselves in serious and committed relationships by then, so one friend bought the other out. During the years they paid a mortgage instead of rent, there was enough equity in the home to pay for a wedding even after the buyout.

I love telling this story. First, I am happy both couples found each other and started their own families. There are also a few lessons to be learned. The first is, a little bit of financial education can go a long way. Second, with the right advisor and some planning, you can buy yourself A LOT of flexibility.

The decision to own versus rent isn't about right or wrong. In my experience, I have observed owning instead of renting fits the goals, objectives, and lifestyle of most of my clients. I may have a little bias, of course. Your life situation and your plans determine which is best for you! That's it. How do you determine if owning is right for you or if renting is a better choice? A little education can make a big difference.

The Financial Comparison

The first place to start is to determine what the cost of ownership is compared to the expense of renting. You can find this Rent vs. Buy calculator on my website at www.brettroessel.com.

We need to start with a few assumptions. Just a quick note that these figures are for illustrative purposes only and should not be taken as financial advice.

Assume your monthly rent payment is $1700 and that your landlord will increase your rent by 1% every year. This figure is probably closer to 3% annually to cover inflation, but we'll demonstrate using a conservative estimate.

Then, suppose you are looking to buy a home for $350,000 which will cost an additional $900 per year for maintenance. Also assume the value of the home will average 3.5% growth every year. Let's just compare what renting would look like over 10 years compared to owning your home for 10 years (years before selling) where the selling cost is the commission to be paid when you sell the home.

We will use 3% as the mortgage interest rate and a 25-year amortization (these figures are for illustrative purposes only to demonstrate the concept).

Input Information

Rent Information

Monthly Rent:	1,700.00	$
Annual Rent Increase:	1.000	%

Property Information

Home Value:	350,000.00	$
Annual Maintenance:	900.00	$
Annual Appreciation:	3.500	%
Years Before Sell:	10	Yrs
Selling Cost:	6.000	%

Loan Information

Amount:	350,000.00	$
Interest Rate:	3.000	%
Length:	25	Yrs

When you compare the total cost of renting over 10 years with the total cost of ownership, you get a really good perspective about whether to rent or buy.

The average monthly rent payment of $1778 includes the 1% annual inflation increase compared to the monthly home ownership costs of $1731, which includes the mortgage payment and annual maintenance costs over 10 years. Immediately, you notice the cost of renting compared to the cost of ownership is almost the same on a monthly basis.

Remember the rule of 72 from Chapter One? The value of your home will grow over time. At the end of 10 years, you will have over $229K MORE by owning your home compared to renting. For roughly the same monthly payment!

Financial Analysis		
	Rent	Buy (Am. Table)
Total Maintenance :	$0.00	$9,000.00
Total Payments :	$213,429.14	$207,763.11
Average Monthly Payment :	$1,778.58	$1,731.36
Monthly Rent Savings :		$-47.22
Total Rent Savings :		$-5,666.03
House Appreciation Value :		$493,709.57
Proceeds Minus Costs :		$464,086.99
Loan Balance :		$240,160.52
Equity Appreciation :		$223,926.47
Home Purchase Benefits :		$229,592.50

Are there scenarios when renting is cheaper than the cost of ownership? Absolutely, there is. In this scenario, the break-even point is around seven years. This means if you were to own the home for less than seven years, renting is the better financial option. I love the power of a little financial education. I get to look at scenarios which save my clients hundreds of thousands of dollars.

Is this a little over-simplified? Yes. There are many factors which will affect the comparison of renting versus owning. That's why it is so important to meet with a mortgage professional to discuss your unique situation and find out what those figures look like for you.

The financial comparison is only one aspect of comparing renting to owning. There are many other reasons that favor owning or renting.

Your Big Asset is likely the single biggest purchase in your lifetime. If you are one of the precious few, you may have the opportunity to buy another home because your family is growing, you want a vacation home, you're looking for an income property or you are ready to retire and want to downsize. Whatever your reasons, this knowledge will live with you forever. That's why I am so excited that you are reading this book. I know whatever you learn here, you will be able to pass along to your friends and family. You will be able to teach your children (if kids are a part of your life right now or may be in the future). That's the kind of generational impact I aspire to have.

There are many reasons beyond the cost of ownership you should consider in choosing to buy a home.

Pros of Owning Your Home

Increasing Net Worth

The ability to increase your personal net worth is a tangible, financial benefit to buying your home. Your net worth is the difference between what you would own if you sold everything and what you owe. In other words, if you were to sell all of your assets (home, car, artwork, investments, etc.) and use the money to pay off all of your debts (mortgage, credit cards, personal loans, etc.) then you would either have some money left over or you would still owe money.

You have a positive net worth when you have money left over and a negative net worth if you don't have enough to pay your debts. When you buy a home, at least in Canada, you will likely increase your net worth over time. We say you are building equity. Remember in Chapter Two when we talked about how real estate generally appreciates in value over time? As that happens, you are building equity.

> **Learning Lesson**
> 'Homeowner's Equity' is often referred to the difference between the current market value of the home and the mortgage balance.
>
> An alternative definition of equity is the difference between the current market value of the home and how much you paid for it. This definition is more in line with the proper definition of profit.

If Net Worth = Assets - Debts,

home ownership helps you increase your net worth in three ways:

- The home appreciates in value (increases the value of your assets)
- You pay down your mortgage (decreases the value of your debts)
- Both

You could even look at your mortgage as a forced savings plan! There are very few purchases a person can make which will have that kind of impact on your financial well-being.

Permanent Shelter

As long as you continue to make your mortgage payments, no one can take your home away from you. You own it. You own the dirt, the garage, the backyard deck, the condo, the apartment. If someone attempted to take that away from you, they have to take you to court because of some other obligations which may have been overlooked. That is a big difference from the challenges a renter can face (more about this later in the chapter).

Owning your home ultimately provides you a permanent shelter. You will always have that for you and your family. My clients take a ton of comfort in knowing their children aren't going to go to sleep without a roof over their heads.

Emergency Fund

Where does a rent payment go after it's given to a landlord? Who knows! Presumably, they use it to pay the mortgage or financing they have in place. Where does a mortgage payment go when you pay it to your lender? Part of the payment goes toward interest and the other part goes towards paying down the principal. When you pay a mortgage payment on your home, the payment doesn't go into the nether, never to be seen again.

Over time, you ACTUALLY do see the principal reduction on your annual mortgage statement. Most banks set up online access to your mortgage account and you can see every transaction in real-time. So, I still haven't answered your question. How does owning my home somehow provide me with an emergency fund?

There are several strategies which enable you to access the repaid principal of your mortgage. First, take a look at how a mortgage is structured. At the beginning, the majority of your payment (weekly, bi-weekly, monthly, etc.) goes to pay the interest. As the mortgage continues, a larger portion of the regular payment goes towards the principal until the mortgage is eventually paid.

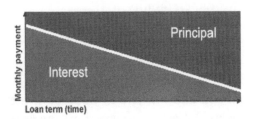

43

Now, back to the emergency-fund question. There are mechanisms in place which enable you to access the principal (more on these in the next chapter). In effect, the equity you have in your home can be used as an emergency fund. What kinds of emergencies can you think of?

- ○ ... Furnace breaks down
- ○ ... Death of a family member
- ○ ... Illness
- ○ ... Car needs repairs
- ○ ... University tuition

There are thousands of scenarios where this might be useful. However, it is also a very dangerous benefit in home ownership and requires responsible decision-making. You work hard to diligently pay down your mortgage and having access to this sum of money can be quite tempting for frivolous items. I am not here to suggest which uses of an emergency fund like this are good or bad. This is just to provide some education on what options exist to put YOU in a position to make informed and competent decisions about your financial future.

Boost Your Credibility

Owning your home has a residual effect of increasing your credibility. Right or wrong. Love it or hate it. Our society simply puts a higher value on owning lucrative assets. Being a homeowner appears to add more credibility than other assets of equal or greater value. You may have a portfolio of investments in stocks and bonds which are worth much more than the average real-estate purchase. Your status as a homeowner would still mean more to your credibility.

There is a greater sense of stability which home ownership signifies. For creditors, they consider home ownership as part of their 'Character' analysis in the *5C's of Credit* (coming up in Chapter Five). To put this bluntly, creditors will know where to find you if they have trouble collecting. Employers look at home ownership as a signal of permanence.

That may not be the case for many people, including you, but it is the

perception of others we all interact with everyday.

The other element of credibility is that most are aware, or at least believe, there is a fairly strict due-diligence process involved in getting approved for and funded to buy a home. Many people trust that the lenders did their homework on you as a borrower and put some faith in their assessment. If you were able to qualify to buy a home, you must have some redeeming qualities.

Side note: That is why the crash in 2008 was so damaging. ONE of the contributing factors was that many mortgages were approved and funded with very little due diligence, which affected pretty much everyone in North America.

Owning a home has very real and tangible financial and non-financial benefits. However, it's not all roses and rainbows and there are other considerations facing a would-be homebuyer.

Con's of Owning Your Home

Everything which starts new doesn't stay new. And anything which is old will eventually need to be replaced. The TRUE cost of ownership extends long after the closing documents are signed, possession and titles are transferred, and the euphoria of a major life change has worn off. Statistics Canada reported that the average household paid over $1000 per month toward shelter costs and ranged between $697-$1366 per month, depending on where you lived[ix]. And these are 2011 figures! They have no doubt increased since then. Here is a list of typical monthly housing expenses in the U.S.[x]

45

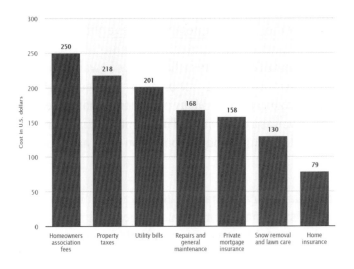

These figures may vary somewhat in Canada, though I feel they are fairly representative in their amounts and spread. The point here is there are many after-sale expenses put onto the homeowners and MOST people do not even consider them prior to purchasing their home. Now that you have this information, you won't make that mistake.

Transaction Costs

Homeowners are required to pay more than the purchase price of the property. These are several expenses that the homeowner is responsible for just to complete the purchase:

Home Inspection	Appraisal
Notary Fees	Legal Fees
Sales Taxes	Transfer Fees

These fees vary by region and provider. They are often referred to as closing costs, but not every lender or broker defines closing costs in the same way. It is very important to investigate all of the extra expenses which need to be paid and how they are to be paid. For some of these expenses, the purchaser must pay out-of-pocket and others are actually deducted from the proceeds of the mortgage. It is the homeowner's responsibility to find out these details and to work with a professional who can detail all of these in advance with a reasonable estimation.

Upkeep & Maintenance

There can be an endless list of maintenance items in a home. A few of the more common items include:

- ○ Landscaping or lawn maintenance
- ○ Snow removal
- ○ Cleaning service
- ○ Repairs and home improvement
- ○ Maintenance products (garden products, furnace filters)
- ○ Contingency fund

Insurance: Property & Mortgage

Although insurance is not isolated to homeowners alone (renters may also carry certain types of insurances), there are certain types of insurances homeowners are obligated to carry.

Property Insurance - Lenders will require specific insurance coverages to protect the asset they are using as security on the mortgage. Insurance coverage may include protection against fire, floods, tornados, or hurricanes (depending on where you live), landslides and other types of risks.

Mortgage Insurance - In Canada, mortgages financed with less than a 20% down payment must insure the mortgage for risk of default. This can either be paid up-front or be built into the mortgage payment.

Title Insurance - Protection of the title of the property from fraud, defects and encroachments. This is not a requirement but may be in the best interests of the homeowner.

I will cover insurances in more detail in Chapter Six.

Property Taxes

Property taxes are the main revenue source for most municipalities. Taxes are levied by the city in which you live and are based on the assessed value of the home. The assessed value of your home is a reasonable estimation of the market value of what the home would sell for on a specific date. The estimation is calculated by the municipality calculating the tax assessment.

Many, if not most, municipalities use the Mill Levy method to calculate the tax using the assessed value.

The mill levy is simply the tax rate levied on your property value, with one mill representing one-tenth of one cent. So, for $1,000 of assessed property value, one mill would be equal to $1. Tax levies for each tax jurisdiction in an area are calculated separately, and then all the levies are added together to determine the total mill rate for an entire region. Generally, the city, county, and school district each have the power to levy against the properties in their boundaries. So, each entity would calculate its required mill levy, and it would all be tallied up to equal the total mill levy[xi].

Every municipality has its own means and methods. Be sure to contact your city government to get the exact calculations for your home.

Rental Property

Your next home may not be your primary residence. Perhaps you choose to buy an income property and rent it out to others. Not only will you have all of the concerns just mentioned above, you will have other considerations, as well.

Your first concern will be how long your rental is vacant. A vacant property does not generate any cash flow through rental income and the homeowner must go out-of-pocket to stay current with the mortgage.

Filling a vacant property requires tenants. There is an entire process to attracting and qualifying tenants. Though it is not my intention to provide a whole lesson on real estate investing (that's not my expertise), I felt it is worth mentioning because I have many clients who choose to buy a second, third or fourth property as investments. Obstacles with tenants include, but are not limited to:

- Timely rent payments
- Care and attention to the property
- Regular upkeep
- Getting along with the neighbors

I've included this discussion as part of the cons of home ownership to provide you some information and not necessarily to scare you. As I mentioned previously, I feel home ownership is a far more attractive strategy than renting in most cases. I also feel an enlightened mind needs not to fear. The more knowledge and education we have about a topic, the less we have to worry about. These events only become a problem when we don't expect them.

You may find this really interesting. The Pros and Cons of renting are almost the polar opposite of the Pros and Cons of owning a home.

"My fleas don't pay any rent and they
have loud parties that keep me awake
all night. I want to have them evicted!"

Pros of Renting

Maintenance is the Landlord's Responsibility

The maintenance and upkeep are usually the landlord's responsibility. The definition of *maintenance* differs between landlords and tenants and should be defined in the rental agreement. Typically, day-to-day or week-to-week maintenance such as cutting the grass, removing snow and paying utilities are the responsibility of the renter. Major repairs such as roofing, painting, appliances, electrical and plumbing are the responsibility of the landlord. Rental agreements can be negotiated on just about any term imaginable as long as both sides feel they are reasonable.

Many owners will hire property managers to take care of the business of the rental property. Quite often, even the day-to-day maintenance is done for you, the cost of which is included in the rent. One of the pros of renting is you only really need to remember to lock the door and pay the rent. It can be virtually hassle-free when you get signed into a good agreement.

Free to Move

The second biggest reason people rent is the freedom to move when they want. Other than the exit clauses of a rental or lease agreement, which might bind a renter to a place for a period of time, there really is no restriction on how long you have to stay in any one place. There are still strategies for arranging an early exit, even when there is an agreement in place for a minimum time frame. Where ownership comes with an anchor, renting is free from this restriction.

Renting is an attractive living arrangement for people who move frequently. A renter may need to move every couple of years for their job. They may prefer the variety of living in many different places. Or they may simply take comfort in knowing if they don't like their current living arrangements, they can change them with relative ease.

Easier to Qualify

Qualifying for a rental agreement is considerably easier than qualifying for a mortgage. This is likely the biggest attraction for people to rent. A renter will usually still need to pass a credit review. This is almost certain with sophisticated landlords and will include verifying references, a credit check, income and employment verification along with a security deposit and the first month's rent. Though the process is somewhat similar to qualifying for a mortgage, the scrutiny by landlords is much lighter.

It makes sense, doesn't it? The landlord already owns the property and a renter isn't going to be able to leave with it. They will simply rent it to another person. All they need to be certain of is that you won't destroy the property and you will pay rent on time.

Cons of Renting

Growing Someone Else's Net Worth

What do you think is the number one drawback of renting instead of owning? You guessed it. You are growing someone else's net worth. That's right. Every single rent payment goes toward paying the mortgage the owner has on the property you're renting. For all the benefits this affords the homeowner, is a drawback to the renter.

- The renter does not participate in the growth of property value.
- The renter participates in paying down the mortgage creating equity under someone else's balance sheet.
- Both

Since the equity growth is afforded to the homeowner, renters do not have the luxury of being able to use the home as an emergency fund. Renters must find another way to build their contingency fund through a different savings plan. That's just a really polite way of saying they have to put money away over and above what they pay for rent. That habit may turn out to be very difficult, depending on the renter's lifestyle and location. They may rent in a very affluent neighborhood or have cash flow issues and be unable to save any extra money.

If you are renting, you can visit my website at www.brettroessel.com and perform your personal Own versus Rent calculation to see if owning might be a better financial fit.

Lack of Status

Renting has always carried a slightly lesser status than owning. Don't be upset with me. I didn't make that decision. Most renters are great people and amazing tenants. There are a few who behave poorly and tarnish the image of others. This is where the benefits of renting work against the status of the tenant. The flexibility of not being anchored or having gone through the due diligence of a mortgage application affects the social status of the renter.

In our society, we value things that are scarce. Virtually anyone can rent, so we don't place much value in the ease or abundance of renting. There's nothing exclusive about renting. You might see a status bump if you happen to be renting a very affluent property in a well-to-do neighborhood, but not nearly as much as you would have if you owned that property.

Suffer the Whims of the Landlord

If there are a few bad tenants out there, then there are also bad landlords. I am sure most landlords are great to work with. People are people and they can be unpredictable, have bad days or just be outright crazy. This is one of the drawbacks of renting which has nothing to do with the financial commitments.

Renters have to deal with landlords as much as landlords have to deal with tenants. Even when there is a good relationship between tenant and landlord, it's still an extra step to getting problems handled. The renter may not be responsible for getting a leaky roof fixed, but it can be just as stressful convincing the landlord to take care of it. At least the homeowner can just deal with the problem. A renter has to persuade the landlord to deal with the problem and go out-of-pocket to do it. From the landlord's perspective, when the renter needs them to take care of the roof, the furnace or the plumbing, it's an extreme inconvenience to them, as well as expense. It may not be that easy to get the landlord too excited to get the work done.

This problem is even worse if the landlord hasn't planned very well, built up a contingency fund or is poor at managing their money. Having to suffer the whims of the landlord is a big drawback to renting.

Market Demand

Low vacancy rates are a nightmare situation for renters.

- Finding available space is 10x more difficult
- Landlords can charge a premium on rental rates
- Double-or-triple qualified offers on rental properties (more competing tenants)
- Less incentive to negotiate on non-financial rental terms (e.g. maintenance programs, rent-free periods)

The Globe and Mail ran a story about the low vacancy and high rates in Vancouver, BC. They mentioned a 43-year-old mother who was having extreme difficulty finding a home for her family[xii].

"She's had potential landlords hang up on her and she's been left waiting for them to show up for viewings. She's been asked for criminal-record checks and credit checks. She's found herself amid standing-room-only crowds with people scrambling to get approved for an empty apartment."

Renting versus owning isn't always a matter of choice. For some people, renting is the only choice they have, at least for the time being. Owning a home is not the exclusive club it is made out to be. There are strategies for almost every scenario. The first step is getting the education to decide for yourself. Then take the next step and find out what's right or what's possible for you!

Ideas to Remember

- There is a financial break-even between owning and renting. The exact figure is dependent on your personal situation.
- There are many pros of owning your home, not all of which are financial.
- Cons of ownership include transaction costs, upkeep and maintenance, insurance, property taxes and issues with rental properties
- There are benefits to renting, including no maintenance obligation, the freedom to move and it's easier to qualify.
- Drawbacks to renting include growing someone else's net worth, the lack of status, suffering the whims of the landlord and market demand.
- Some people have no other choice but to rent.

CHAPTER FOUR
CHANGING TIMES OF HOME OWNERSHIP

"Real estate cannot be lost or stolen, nor can it be carried away. Purchased with common sense, paid for in full and managed with reasonable care, it is about the safest investment in the world."

~ Franklin D. Roosevelt

A lot has changed about mortgaging a home since I started my career 20+ years ago. I wouldn't even consider myself the old guy telling stories of how things worked back in the good old days. I just happened to start my career very early and worked my way up. Back at the turn of the millennium (early 2000), there were only a few fixed-interest products and a couple of select terms. In those days, consumers really didn't have a lot of choice regarding financial vehicle or provider. There were only the major banks and just a few emerging unconventional lenders.

Looking back 20 years, there appeared to be a lot more handshake deals based on relationships. The lenders seemed to care a lot more about Character in the *5C's* (the *5C's of Credit* are Character, Collateral, Capacity, Credit, Cash). The number of people who were buying homes was steadily increasing, the economy was strong, and everyone seemed to be making good money. Risk for the lenders appeared to be a lot more predictable.

Then 2009 hit.

You probably remember this financial crisis (*crisis* might be a strong word, in retrospect) blasted the whole world. Nearly every financial institution was rocked and very few economies were left unaffected. Some were hit harder than others. This book is not the time nor place to discuss the causes of the crash in late 2008/early 2009. There are ample resources for you to read about why and how it happened. (As a side note, I really enjoyed the movie *The Big Short*. It provides a very entertaining perspective on the events leading up to the crash. Enjoy it for what it is, a Hollywood movie.)

Looking back on that time, it was actually a small blip by comparison. When we look back over time, we see that the crash of 2009 was relatively short. Take a look at this segment comparing GDP going back to 1970. GDP, or Gross Domestic Product, is one measurement used to gauge the health of an economy. The bar chart along the bottom charts the growth of quarterly GDP. In 2008-2009 we see three consecutive quarters of negative GDP. That means that the economy was experiencing negative growth. In other words, recession.

This period was not as long as the similar experience in the early 90's and definitely did not last as long as that of the early 80's. I am at that wonderful age where I am old enough to remember what times were like during all three! What makes this one a little different is:

○ The length of time since the last recession (almost 20 years)
○ The drop was quite steep compared to those in the past.

You may recall there were significant consecutive drops in all the major trading markets, such as the NYSE, Nasdaq, Dow, TSX, Nikkei and many others. The event itself was short by comparison but has left a much bigger scar than the others.

It has changed how mortgages are regulated and approved.

Since 2009, things have changed a lot…

- ○ Character carries less meaning then Capacity or Credit in the approval process.
- ○ Lenders need more substantial proof of a buyer's creditworthiness.
- ○ Mortgage applicants are scrutinized more than ever.
- ○ Lenders are spending more resources in order to spread their risk and protect themselves.
- ○ Governments are imposing stricter regulations about mortgage terms, approvals, and processing.
- ○ Credit underwriters are relying more on empirical data instead of the credibility of the broker and their client.

Here is why you should care. Whether you are someone who has a mortgage or had one in the past or you are a first-time homebuyer and new to the process, you need to know that the industry has changed. Getting a mortgage is different than the last time you closed on a home.

You might be a first-time homebuyer and be relying on the advice of family or friends who have a mortgage. I can almost guarantee the industry has changed since they last wrote their mortgage, at least at the time of the writing of this book.

The additional scrutiny and regulatory changes have made it difficult to qualify for a mortgage. This has also spawned a massive growth in the number and types of mortgage products available from many different types of lenders, both conventional and unconventional. Researching a mortgage is no longer as simple as going to your bank's website to look at the two or three options they have and comparing them to the same structures at the other banks. There are quite literally several hundred combinations of rates and terms to be combined with other features to customize what you need. Many of these are ONLY available through a professional broker.

The rest of the chapter we will dive into all the considerations a mortgage client needs to know in today's market.

Programs and Products

If you haven't gotten the message yet, a lot has changed for homeowners in the last 15-20 years. New programs have been launched and old programs have been updated. Programs for people new to Canada have been launched and the new homebuyer programs have been revised. A flood of new mortgage products has been introduced by a ton of new competitors.

Traditionally, most homebuyers used to go to their personal banks to shop for a mortgage. Part of it was they already had a relationship there with their existing accounts. They may even know their account manager. The other part of it was there wasn't really any benefit to going to another bank, because they generally offered very similar rate and terms.

Rates and terms have changed. A lot! Today, there are different lenders, spanning from conventional, unconventional, institutional money and private money. For example, I have access to over 35 different lenders, including banks, b-lenders and private moneylenders. That doesn't include any referral arrangements to which I have access. Each lender carries multiple rate and term options:

	Fixed Rate Options	Variable Rate Options
Primary Lenders	10+	2+
Alternative/B-Lenders	7+	2
Private Lenders	3+	0

When you add it all up, there are well over 100 combinations of rate and amortization terms which can be structured from this list. You can imagine how difficult it would be for a homeowner to navigate ALL of the mortgage options available to them.

Now let me complicate this one step further. Out of all the 35+ lenders x the fixed/variable rate options, they all have different qualifying criteria. Some of the lenders will only finance good credit histories, some will take on a few credit blemishes and a few others will finance deeper credit challenges. All the other factors about for which lenders you may be a good fit include:

o Amount of down payment
o Credit score
o Debt service ratios
o Loan to value ratios
o Time on the job
o Type of income

Lastly, there are lenders included in this list which can only be accessed through a professional mortgage broker. Many of these programs are not even available to the retail public. So how is a homeowner expected to navigate this process on top of taking the time and effort to shop for a home they really want to buy?

The short answer is - they need a professional broker.

New to Canada

Qualifying for a mortgage in Canada has its own challenges for current citizens. New immigrants to Canada have twice the level of difficulty when they want to buy a home. Once they get over the shock of the housing prices in most major cities, the three biggest challenges facing immigrants to Canada are:

1. Residence
2. Income Verification
3. Credit History

Income Verification
Credit History

It will be very difficult for immigrants on a temporary work visa to qualify for a mortgage to buy their home. I am not saying it is impossible but is very difficult. Those who have considerable assets who immigrate to Canada have a better chance if they are on a temporary visa. Lenders are typically looking for a minimum of a 35% down payment and evidence of 12 months of mortgage payments on deposit in their Canadian bank account. The catch? Lenders will not include any assets residing outside of Canada in the net worth calculation. Those assets must be in Canada to be included AND need to be here for a minimum of 30 days to comply with Anti-Money Laundering laws.

On the other hand, permanent residents have the same borrowing status as Canadian citizens in the eyes of the lenders. Is there another catch? Yes. It can take an immigrant 6-12 months or longer to get approved for permanent residence. Once received, the new-to-Canada mortgage borrower is reviewed for credit approval in much the same way a Canadian citizen is.

The next challenge then is income verification. Lenders are going to want to know how you earn your income and if you have capacity to pay back a mortgage on time. Income type will have a significant impact on the mortgage approval. Self-employed individuals will need to provide 2 years worth of Canadian self-employment income for verification. Salaried employees may have less of a challenge, though most lenders will want to see a minimum of three-months employment, the exception being corporate relocation programs.

Once residency and income status can be verified, the next challenge is credit history. Since most immigrants to Canada do not have a credit history from lending institutions (I have not met any who have), this can be the biggest challenge to overcome. Lenders are looking for a minimum of a 12-month history on two credit accounts (called trades). However, a good report from an international credit report may be acceptable as part of the application. Ultimately, the lender is trying to determine if you are a good risk.

One element which can sweeten the pot for a lender is mortgage insurance. Mortgage insurance is a government-backed guarantee for the lender, who must meet the insurer's criteria. There is more coming on this topic in Chapter 6.

Here is an excerpt of the qualification criteria with GenWorth Canada, one of Canada's mortgage insurers[xiii].

Borrower Qualification	**Income & Employment** • Standard income and employment verification requirements apply • 3 months minimum full time employment in Canada (borrowers being transferred under a corporate relocation program are exempt) **Credit** • 90.01-95%: International credit report (Equifax or Transunion) demonstrating a strong credit profile OR two (2) alternative sources of credit demonstrating timely payments (no arrears) for the past 12 months. The two alternative sources required are: - Rental payment history - One other alternative source (hydro/utilities, telephone, cable, cell phone and auto insurance) • Up to 90%: Letter of reference from a recognized financial institution OR six (6) months of bank statements from primary account **Down Payment** • Qualified home buyers may use traditional down payment sources including personal savings, non-repayable gift from immediate family member(s), proceeds from sale of property. • 95% LTV, 5% of the down payment must be from own resources • < 95% LTV, the remainder may be gifted from an immediate family member or from a corporate subsidy **Additional Criteria** • Must have immigrated or relocated to Canada within the last 60 months • Must have a valid work permit or obtained landed immigrant status • All debts held outside of the country must be included in the total debt servicing ratio(Rental income earned outside of Canada is to be excluded from the GDS/TDS calculation) • Guarantors are not permitted • Foreign Diplomats who do not pay tax in Canada are ineligible for this program

The feeling you're probably getting is this might be a process worth planning. You are right. Depending on your personal situation, qualifying for a program like this will need to take some planning so the type of residence is verified, income checks out and the credit history can be retrieved OR can be established if none exists.

First Time Home Buyers Plan

In many ways, first-time homebuyers may face similar challenges, though many do not. It really depends where you are in your life journey.

o You may be just starting out on your own. You are beginning your career job and receive a steady income. You may not have much of a credit history and a little bit of savings. Perhaps you are getting a portion of a down payment gifted to you from family.

o Are you well into your career and have been earning a good income for a little while now? Perhaps you have a bit of savings in your bank account and your RRSP's (Registered Retirement Savings Plan) and you are ready to get out of the rental market and join the homeowners club.

o You may have experience owning a home but have been renting for the past few years for one reason or another. Perhaps you have substantial savings in your RRSP and want to get back into owning your home again.

Whatever your story is, you need to know about the Home Buyers Plan (HBP). This program was initiated by the federal government (Canada) in 2006 to assist first-time homebuyers in getting into the market. The program enables a would-be homebuyer to withdraw up to $25,000 from their RRSP tax free to use as part of a down payment on the purchase of a qualified property. The program requires that the withdrawal be paid back every year over a maximum of 15 years.

This is pretty substantial, because participants in this program get the full use of money typically locked up behind a tax barrier. If a homebuyer were to use their RRSP money as a down payment and they were not in the HBP, they would be subject to a withholding tax right at withdrawal, which means they wouldn't be able to use the full $25,000. Then they would need to claim the $25,000 as income that year, which could possibly trigger a tax liability (less the withholding tax) at the end of the tax year.

The HBP is based on a per-person basis. That means any couple who is buying a home can withdraw up to $25,000 each for a total of $50,000. Using this as a 5% down payment may enable you to shop for a home for up to a $1 million selling price.

Straight from the source[xiv]:

Do you meet the RRSP withdrawal conditions?

- You have to be a resident of Canada at the time of the withdrawal.
- You have to receive or be considered to have received, all withdrawals in the same calendar year.
- You cannot withdraw more than $25,000.
- Only the person who is entitled to receive payments from the RRSP can withdraw funds from an RRSP. You can withdraw funds from more than one RRSP as long as you are the owner of each RRSP. Your RRSP issuer will not withhold tax on withdraw amounts of $25,000 or less.
- Normally, you will not be allowed to withdraw funds from a locked-in RRSP or a group RRSP.
- Your RRSP contributions must stay in the RRSP for at least 90 days before you can withdraw them under the HBP. If this is not the case, the contributions may not be deductible for any year.
- Neither you nor your spouse or common-law partner or the related person with a disability that you buy or build the qualifying home for can own the qualifying home more than 30 days before the withdrawal is made.
- You have to buy or build a qualifying home for yourself, for a related person with a disability, or to help a related person with a disability buy or build a qualifying home before October 1st of the year after the year of the withdrawal.
- You have to fill out Form T1036, Home Buyers' Plan (HBP) Request to Withdraw Funds from an RRSP for each eligible withdrawal.

A little-known provision of the Home Buyers Plan is you don't need to be a NEW homebuyer. The way CRA classifies a first-time home buyer is as the following:

> You are considered a first-time home buyer if, in the four-year period, you did not occupy a home that you or your current spouse or common-law partner owned.

If you have owned a home in the past but not within the past four years, you may qualify for the HBP. This can be a very useful program for those who qualify.

Mortgages and Home Equity Line-of-Credit (HELOC)

I briefly discussed mortgages in Chapter One - Financial Literacy, and you may recall that the earliest recorded mortgages date back to 2000 B.C. As a reminder, the definition for mortgage is:

*A legal agreement by which a bank or other creditor lends money at interest
in exchange for taking title of the debtor's property,
with the condition that the conveyance becomes void upon the payment of the debt.*

Reading the definition, it doesn't sound much different than a personal loan to buy a car. Truthfully, there isn't much difference. A lender provides the capital to purchase the property and then registers a claim on that property until the debt is paid. In a car loan, the lender will register a lien, while on real estate, the lender will register a conveyance. Both types of debts have a regular payment schedule over a period of time, which includes interest calculated on the borrowed amount and an annualized rate.

There is one major difference between the two which you must understand. The interest in a mortgage is compounded, while the interest on a loan is simple interest. Simple interest is only calculated on the principal, while compound is interest on interest (see the Rule of 72 in Chapter One). The interest in a mortgage is compounded monthly.

What does that really mean to you as a homeowner buying their Big Asset? Take a look at the chart below, which illustrates the repayment of the mortgage, also known as the amortization schedule.

As you make your regular payments on your mortgage, part of your payment goes towards interest and the rest to pay down the principal. The earlier payments are mostly interest and the later payments are mostly principal. As you can see, the crossover point, where more of your payment starts to pay down the principal is just a little over halfway. This is a very simplified example and many factors may affect this repayment schedule:

- o Variable interest rates
- o Additional principal pre-payments
- o Mortgage rescheduling
- o Accelerated payment schedules
- o Refinancing

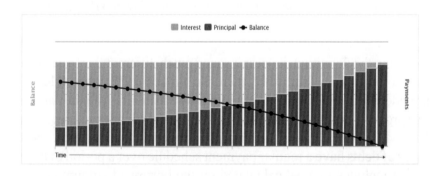

To put the compound interest subject into perspective, let's compare a mortgage versus a loan. The illustration above shows a $500,000 mortgage paid monthly and amortized over 30 years with an annual interest rate of 3.0%. The total interest costs over the lifetime of the mortgage without any changes would be $466,278.

Compare that to a simple interest loan for $500,000 paid monthly over 30 years at a 3% interest rate. Any idea how much the total interest costs would be? The total interest on this debt would be $258,887.

Principal Borrowed	$500,000
Annual Interest Rate	3%
Payment Frequency	Monthly

Mortgage Interest Paid	$466,278
Loan Interest Paid	$258,887
Compounding Difference	+$207,391

That represents a difference of $207,391! That is the power of compound interest. Unfortunately, this is an example of when compounding works against us and in favor of the lender. Do you think it is important to understand how these vehicles work? Of course. Do you also think it is also important to put together strategies to reduce this interest expense as much as possible while keeping as much flexibility as possible? Absolutely.

Now that you have a base understanding of what mortgages are, and how they work, they have changed somewhat since the early 12th century. Mortgages have evolved along with changes in our economies. The way we make money, the way we spend money and how we save money.

There are a lot of conditions which effect which mortgage products lenders are willing to offer. And I mean A LOT. I could base an entire a career and a couple of PhDs analyzing this industry. I like things simple. Borrowers need to borrow, lenders need to lend, and investors need to invest. Product offerings are a constant flux of what each of those groups wants, needs and is willing to spend money to do.

In understanding how mortgages have changed and how it affects you, the most publicized change in mortgages are the rates offered. Here is an interesting recounting of rates on 30-year, fixed-rate mortgages[xv].

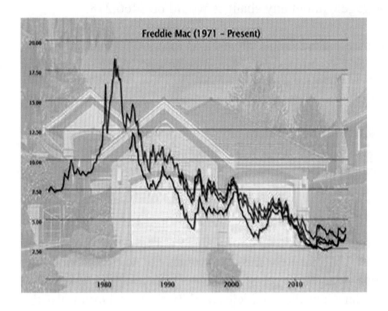

Freddie Mac (1971 - Present)

You are either one of those who have lived through the interest rate peaks in the 1980's, know someone who has or have at least heard about them. Depending on your source, mortgage interest rates in the 80's clipped up over 21% at their maximum. Compare that to rates today which, at the time of writing this book, hover between 2.5-4% for fixed and variable-rate mortgages. What a massive difference. Interest rates have changed a lot over the last few decades. They continue to change as our economy and consumer needs change.

Another major shift in mortgages is in the terms offered. Back in those high-interest periods of the 80's and even into the early 90's, 30-year, fixed-rate mortgages were the norm. If we go back prior to the 1930's, mortgages were typically only five years. At that time, property ownership was a luxury of the wealthy and most had substantial cash or other assets with which to buy their property. Around 1934 saw the establishment of the FHA, or Federal Housing Administration (United States), to protect lenders and reduce the risk of default on payments. The 30-year mortgage was born[xvi].

Then 2008 brought substantial rule changes to mortgage qualifications[xvii].

Prior to the first rule change:

o No down payment required – 100% finance.
o Maximum amortization was 40 years.
o Refinance up to 95% the value of your home.

Fall 2008:

o Reduction of maximum amortization from 40 years to 35 years.
o 100% financing was eliminated. (However, you could still use a Cash Back Mortgage for a down payment).

Spring 2010:

o Stricter rental-property guidelines. The amount of rent for income/debt servicing purposes was reduced from 80% to 50%.
o A Mortgage Qualifying Rate was introduced for all insured mortgages on all variable-terms and all fixed-rate mortgage terms four years and less. (five-year fixed-rate mortgages were still allowed to qualify at the contract rate).
o Rental Mortgage down-payment minimum was raised from 10% to 20%.
o Insured refinances reduced from 95% Loan-to-Value to 90%.

Spring 2011:

o Insured Home Equity Lines-of-Credit discontinued.
o Insured refinances further reduced from 90% Loan-to-Value to 85%.
o Maximum amortizations lowered further from 35 years to 30 years.

Summer 2012:

- ○ Implementation of a New Gross Debt Service Ratio maximum of 39%.
- ○ Refinance Loan-to-Value reduced further from 85% to 80%.
- ○ Maximum amortization reduced from 30 years to 25 years for insured mortgages.

Fall 2016:

- ○ Mortgage Insurance limited to purchase prices not exceeding $999,999.
- ○ Insured refinances were eliminated altogether.
- ○ High-ratio qualifications using the benchmark rate introduced.

Jan 2018:

- ○ All conventional mortgages will need to qualify with their own stress test or the contract rate +2.0%. This means if the five-year fixed rate is 3.49%, you would have to qualify at a rate of 5.49%.

When you consider all of these rule changes over a span of 10 years (most of which came in the last few years) and many others which have been left out of this discussion, how is an average homebuyer supposed to keep up so they can make a good financial decision in their own best interests?

My point of going so deep on this discussion is not to scare or discourage you. I feel it's important to pass on to you some of the knowledge I have learned so you can understand how to make a good decision for yourself. That doesn't mean you have to become the expert on mortgages, their history and all their financial levels just so you can buy a home. It does mean you need to become more informed when you are making one of the biggest financial decisions in your life. So the answer to the question in the last paragraph is--get help from a competent mortgage professional.

"The only thing that is constant is change."
~ *Heraclitus*

Mortgages have evolved a ton over time, but it's not because lenders feel like making changes. They respond competitively to the needs of their potential customers as much as any business. What has changed which would force lenders to come up with new and innovative methods to mortgage home purchases?

	1979	2017	Change
Minimum Wage	$3.05	$11.60 / hr	+2.8x
Average Annual Income (Individual)	$22,986 / yr	$51,000 / yr	+1.2x
Housing Prices	$70,830	$495,000	+6.0x

* Multiple data sources

Take a look at the change in average incomes for Canadians from 1979 to 2017. Minimum wage has changed almost tripled and the average annual income for an individual is just over double in the same period. Now look at the average price of a home in Canada. The difference is 6x! Do you think there is an economic response for lenders to develop new mortgage programs so people can continue to choose to buy homes?

Remember, lenders need to lend to make money and investors need to invest.

Before you jump up and down about the figures, there are many sources of data that can be used; each of which has its own criteria, depending on the source. Of course, there are a ton of factors which feed into this machine. One of the biggest mechanisms for these types of changes is supply and demand.

I am not an economist, but I understand that when supply goes down or demand goes up, prices increase. What do you think happened in the 1930's that had an impact on demand for buying homes? You guessed it--lenders provided mortgage products buyers could afford at their income level. This led to an ever-increasing flow of people who want to buy their homes. Today, lenders are continuously launching new and specialized products to appeal to different types of borrowers while still managing their risk.

Looking forward, I also feel we are primed for another major shift in financial services, especially in mortgages. We are starting to see major disruption coming from the Financial Technologies (FinTech) industry which is bringing in customers who have been un-bankable (which is most of the world, by the way) together with people who have some extra cash they would be willing to invest in micro loans and doing it in a way which can predict risk 10-20x more accurately than legacy systems.

I won't go into any more detail about my thoughts and feelings on this, but if history tells us anything, it is that people always seem to find a way to make things work.

Let's explore this trend of rising purchase prices for homes. Although you have no control over this, I feel it is important enough to mention. The average home prices have been steadily rising across Canada since as far back as you care to measure. The Canada New Housing Price Index is a good indicator of what is happening. It measures the price comparisons of new homes with the same specifications year over year[xviii].

I don't have to be an economic genius to see the trade is steadily upward dating back to 1981. Remember the housing boom in 2008 and the subsequent economic crash in 2009. They appear as little blips looking back on them, just as they looked when we discussed the GDP earlier in this chapter.

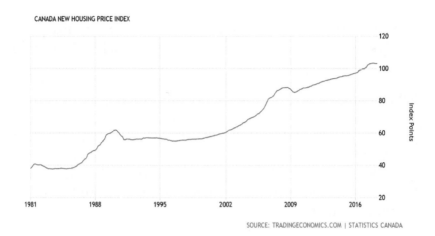

CANADA NEW HOUSING PRICE INDEX

SOURCE: TRADINGECONOMICS.COM | STATISTICS CANADA

Here are some questions I would be asking myself....

Is this trend more likely or less likely to continue long-term?

Does this mean I need to get in as early as I can if buying a home is something I intend to do?

What are the other factors affecting how home prices will behave?

What three or four pieces of information do I really need to put myself in a good position to buy my home?

How do I get in touch with the right professionals who can help guide me through my decision?

Aging Buyers

The changing trends in home ownership also include some likely and unlikely scenarios. First-time homebuyers are getting older, while the age of homes is getting younger. Say that five times fast.

The Statistics Canada 2016 Census reported that Millennials have a lower home ownership at the age of 30 than the Baby Boomers did at the same age[xix]. Why this comparison? Both generations appear to be similar in size. At the age of 30, approximately 50% of Millennials lived in their own home, compared to 55% of Baby Boomers when they were 30 years old. Now is this a function of different economies or just a difference in generational culture?

I would suggest it is a blend of both. I don't have any qualifications to discuss the differences of habits between Millennials and Baby Boomers, so let's review the economies of the time. When Baby Boomers turned 30 in 1981, incomes were high relative to housing prices and new mortgage products were being introduced to make buying a home much more affordable. As we have already seen, housing prices have outgrown incomes by as much as 4x. The result is that Millennials will need to qualify for higher mortgages with larger down payments using comparatively less income.

Single or Joint Applicant

When you consider the trends in housing prices, incomes, and financial regulations, it should be no surprise that I do not submit many applications which include only one borrower. Most, if not all, of the applicants I see either have a spouse with whom they are buying their home, or they have access to a co-signer. That is not to say there is no hope for a single applicant to get into a home. It's just a matter of managing expectations.

That could be said about this entire book so far. Getting the right education about all the factors you should consider when buying your home is about managing your expectations--about risk, approval, minimum requirements, long-term outcomes, or short-term goals.

Who is more likely to get into a 6000 square foot mansion for $5 million--the double-income family who grosses one million dollars in income and has a $750,000 down payment, or the university student who just finished school and is about to start their career at his first fulltime job? Both types of people have the same objective of buying a home. The goal, then, is to figure out what they really want and how to get there.

The gift of financial education you have just given yourself over the last four chapters is more than a business graduate will receive in a four-year degree. Congratulations. Now I have a challenge for you. How will you put this information to use in your life and with whom will you share it?

Ideas to Remember

o   The economic downturn of 2009 required the mortgage industry to adapt.

o   Character as part of the *5C's* carries less weight in the credit application than it used to.

o   There are hundreds of combinations of mortgage programs between the different types of lenders, the rates they offer and the terms.

o   Homebuyers need competent and knowledgeable professionals to help them navigate the mortgage process and make good financial decisions.

o   Immigrants to Canada may be eligible for a qualified mortgage under the New-to-Canada program.

o   The New-to-Canada program relies on three factors: Type of residency, income verification and international credit history.

o   The First -ime Home Buyers Plan permits the use of a tax-free RRSP withdrawal for up to $25,000 per individual.

o   You can be considered a first-time home buyer if you have not owned your home in the past four years.

o   Mortgage products have changed substantially in the last 30 years, including rates, terms and other conditions.

o   HELOC may be a powerful and dangerous alternative or supplement to mortgages.

o   Incomes have not kept pace with the growth of housing prices since 1979.

o   Selling prices for new homes have been on a steady climb since 1981.

o   Fewer Millennials are buying homes compared to their Baby Boomer counterparts at the same age.

o   Changing trends are making owning a home as an individual increasingly difficult but not impossible.

CHAPTER FIVE:
BUYING THE GARAGE FOR THE CAR!

"The ache for home lives in all of us, the safe place where we can go as we are and not be questioned."

~ Maya Angelou

I love this quote by Maya Angelou. I feel it's a more eloquent way of saying *home is where the heart is.* There are very few things a person can buy which may get them so wrapped up emotionally and have such a lasting impact on them. Buying a home is unique in that way. Since buying a home can be such an emotional journey, it makes sense to take a step back, set aside your emotions and look at a practical approach to buying and mortgaging your home.

That's why I like to say, "Buy the garage before the car." You'll thank me later.

I recall a couple of years ago when I was working with this particular client. They were a really nice couple and were looking at their options to stop renting and buy their home. So, they took prudent action--they called me to look at their mortgage options before they went shopping for a house. I took their application, and everything looked pretty good. They had good household income, long tenures at both of their jobs and a down payment. I was able to get them preapproved for their mortgage without much interference. It was about a week after I gave them the good news that I find out they'd decided to go buy a new car. They had pretty good credit, so they had little trouble getting approved for the car loan. The problem was that the new $600 per month loan payment put their debt service out of reach. In other words, they could then only qualify for a smaller mortgage.

The unfortunate news is that this happens more often than you would think. The upside is there are still options in cases such as these which usually come with higher fees and rates. The question you need to ask yourself is, "How bad do you want this home and at what cost are you willing to pay?"

> ### Learn the Terms
> Gross Debt Service Ratio (GDSR) - the ratio of total monthly payment obligations divided by the gross monthly income expressed as a percentage (%).
>
> GDSR = Principal + Interest + Taxes + Heat + [condo fees excluding heat]
> ───────────────────────────────────────
> Gross Monthly Income
>
> The target ratio is 35% or lower.

Thankfully, they were able to find a home and qualify for the mortgage amount they needed. Admittedly, as they got caught up in the emotion of getting preapproved for a mortgage and began shopping for a home, they let it take control and went looking for a car for some immediate gratification. There is nothing wrong with buying the new car and enjoying all the luxuries life has to offer and that you can afford. But this type of journey requires a plan.

There is too much at stake for you. This is your Big Asset and you are getting into a purchase for the next 25-30 years and at the cost of hundreds of thousands of dollars or more. Even if you don't intend to stay in the home you plan to buy right now or the home you plan to buy next, this decision will affect what you may do and how you can do it for all future homes you look to buy. It doesn't matter if this is your first home or your fifth. Conditions are constantly changing. Lenders are constantly changing. Governments are constantly changing the regulations. Your life situation is constantly changing.

A few hours of planning to save you a lifetime of hassle doesn't seem like that bad of a trade-off.

Buy the garage before the car. That is meant both literally and figuratively.

You have decided you want to buy a home and need a mortgage to do it. What's next? In the rest of this chapter, I will go into detail about developing your plan. Your plan will need to answer questions like:

○ Is this your primary home or secondary home?
○ How much down payment will you commit?
○ Do you need to insure your mortgage? Should you insure it anyway?
○ What is your 90-day history of your bank account?
○ What is your qualifying criteria (*5C's*)?
○ What type of pre-payment options do you need?

Your plan is your road map to setting expectations. Some of the biggest battles in mankind were caused because of unmet expectations. Well sort of. There is frustration and then there is the reality gap. I love this formula for calculating unmet expectations[xx]:

Higher Expectation - Lesser Observation = Frustration

I think we all deal with this at some point in our lives. Some more than others. We have high expectations of ourselves and of those we love. Not everyone will live up to those high expectations. I would even venture to say if you are living up to every one of your expectations, you're selling yourself short. The frustration from not meeting these high expectations only sets in when we have lesser observation. We are simply not aware anything else could happen. That is frustrating.

Then there is the reality gap:

Higher Expectation - Lesser Reality = Reality Gap

The only difference is that we are more in tune with our environment or, as the formula states it, our reality. There does not need to be frustration with unmet expectations. We just need to be in sync with our reality. And that's why developing this plan is so important.

Your plan enables you to get in sync with your reality. How frustrated do you think the couple who bought the car and almost ruined their mortgage approval were? Do you think if they would have included a new car in their plan that they would have felt the reality gap instead of frustration? Absolutely.

Up until this point in the book, I have written about financial history, philosophy, mindset and a few technical details. All of this has been to prepare you for what's next. The remainder of the book is going to a combination of *how-to* and *why-should-you*. All the technical information you are going to be able to use for the rest of your life are in these next few chapters. I am excited for you to read on. One of the reasons I started this career is because of the impact I can have on families and the happiness they experience when they buy their homes. Through this book, I get to be a part of your journey.

Develop a Plan

By now, you are probably pretty excited. You have decided you are going to buy a home! I see people get just as excited over their fourth or fifth home as they do their first. Before you jump into your car and start touring open houses with your Realtor, you need to develop a plan for how you're going to mortgage whatever home you decide to close on.

Do you remember PEMDAS? This is how order of operations is taught in Grade Four math. It stands for:

Parentheses
Exponents
Multiplication
Division
Addition
Subtraction

When I went to school it was BEDMAS where the '**B**' stood for brackets and we calculated division before multiplication. Whichever way you learned you understand that some steps need to be completed before others. That's why we develop the plan, so that we know which steps we need to complete and when they need to be done. This way, we can manage our expectations and avoid frustration. The ultimate goal here is to get a mortgage approved and funded as quickly and easily as possible.

Step 1 - Will this Purchase be Your Primary Home or Secondary (e.g. Rental, Vacation Property, Investment)?

This first step is actually quite simple. Remember I like simple, right? The first decision you need to make is if this home you are buying is your primary residence or if it's a secondary residence. It's so simple it doesn't even feel like a decision, but the rest of the plan relies pretty heavy on the outcome in this step.

Primary Home

You have decided this is going to be your primary home. Perhaps you're a first-time homebuyer or you're selling your current home to buy another one. You might even be keeping your current home as a rental property and move into a new home as your primary. Whatever your situation is, I am glad we are doing this plan! This is going to help put you in the best possible financial outcome long after you have taken possession of your new home.

○ Requires a minimum of 5% down payment

- Also requires default insurance with down payments less than 20%
- All other general conditions

Secondary Home

You have decided to up your home ownership game to the next level and buy a secondary home as a vacation home, rental property or investment property.

- Vacation homes may still qualify for the minimum 5% down payment, though there are conditions around this option.
- Rental or investment properties require a minimum 20% down payment.
- Same qualifying conditions as buying a primary home.

Rental Properties

- Lenders will build in a rental offset.
- Will use between 50-80% of the rental as income.
- Some lenders will permit between 4-10 rental properties and still consider them residential though it differs between lenders. The common average is five properties before getting reclassified as commercial business.

Other Investment Properties

- Investment properties such as flips or wholesale are treated as a business by lenders and cross the line into commercial business.
- Much different process with other qualifying criteria.

Step 2 - Purchase Price

This is a really fun part of the plan, as we sit together and dream about the type of home we want to buy. I get to have amazing discussions with my clients about where they want to live, what kind of yard they want, what the kitchen should look like, if they're going to save a room for a den or office, will they develop the basement or find a home with a finished basement. I love this exercise because we all get to dream a little.

This is also a time to set expectations. The mortgage we qualify for will play a deciding role in the budget with which you are comfortable shopping. Most of my clients are reasonable enough to know if they will be able to afford a $3 million home or a $300,000 home. The difference between a $600,000 home and a $400,000 home may limit the cities in which you can shop or the areas in which you want to live. Here are my suggestions when setting a purchase price for your shopping budget:

i.   Set the low-budget range -The low-end is the absolute minimum you feel you will need to find the home with which you can be happy. It should be able to cover your second or third choice areas and the absolute must-haves in your home (e.g. two bedrooms, two bathrooms, a yard, etc.).

ii.   Set the upper-budget range - The upper budget range is the absolute max you are willing to spend to get everything you want, including location, amenities, layout, appliances, development and all of those other items we listed in the dreaming stage I mentioned earlier.

iii.   Set a renovation budget - Set an approximate budget for how much you would be willing to spend on renovations if that is something you require.

iv.   Column of Wants and Must Haves - Write a line down the center of a piece of paper. On the top of the left side write *Wants* and on the top of the right side write *Must Haves*. Start to fill each column with all the attributes you are looking for in your home, with the things you want but can live without on the left side and the absolutely-cannot-live-without things on the right. This will also be a great list you can share with your Realtor when you start to look for your home.

> **Did you know?**
> You can get renovations pre-approved within your mortgage as 'purchase +
> improvements'. The program is designed to give you options to change the
> kitchen, replace the flooring, build a garage or any other improvements you
> can think of.
>
> This strategy is particularly effective when you found the near-perfect
> house. Instead of going out of pocket to renovate the bathroom after you
> purchased the property, you can have the cost of construction already built
> in to your mortgage payment provided you meet all the qualification
> requirements.

Step 3 - General Conditions

You are likely already familiar with the documents needed to satisfy
general conditions, though you may not have heard them called that
before. General conditions include...

- Down Payment
- Income & Employment
- Qualifying Criteria (*5C's*)

The down payment and income/employment verifications will need to
come from you in acceptable forms of documentation while the qualifying
criteria is a high-level approach the lenders will use to make a decision on
your mortgage application.

Down Payment

The down payment is required on every mortgage. As part of the general conditions, the down payment plays a few different roles in your plan. The size of the down payment affects the Loan-to-Value, which in turn also determines if default insurance is required. In addition, the down payment influences the payment in the mortgage schedule, which in turn determines your TDSR.

It is the scenario around the property which determines how much of a down payment is required (e.g. primary or secondary home). The down payment is calculated as a percentage of the purchase price of the home. For example, a 5% down payment on a home on the purchase agreement for $300,000 will be $15,000; a 20% down payment equates to $60,000.

Learn the Terms

Loan to Value (LTV) - the ratio of the portion of the property fair market value that is financed by the mortgage expressed as a percentage (%).

$$LTV = \frac{Fair\ Market\ Value\ (FMV)}{Total\ Outstanding\ Mortgage}$$

A home that is valued at $300,000 with an outstanding mortgage of $285,000 has an LTV of 95%. In the same way, a 20% down payment on a mortgage will have an LTV of 80%.

A down payment which is less than 20% is considered a high-ratio mortgage, or insurable, and default insurance is required. Default insurance is covered in the next chapter. Just know when default insurance is required or you opt into it, it the premium is added to the mortgage, increases your mortgage payment and can affect your TDSR.

Down payments which are more than 20% are called conventional, uninsured or insurable mortgages. When the LTV is 80% or less, default insurance is not required, though there may be situations where it makes sense for you to opt-in to the insurance and pay the premium. More on that later.

INTERESTING NOTE: Have you ever wondered why you can get a cheaper rate with a smaller down payment? Especially since larger down payments reduce the risk to the lender. The lenders may choose to insure your mortgage on the backend, which means they are paying the default insurance premium. To cover the additional expense, the lender will charge a higher rate on uninsured mortgages. This makes them more attractive to other financial institutions, who buy bundles of these mortgages from lenders.

<u>Source of Your Down Payment</u>

Savings are not the only way to produce a down payment for your home purchase. There are a few different ways to raise the money you need for your down payment.

Whatever your source for the down payment, you must either be able to verify the 90-day history or provide an acceptable proof of source for the lenders. In other words, the lenders will only accept a down payment you can prove you have had in place for 90+ days or be able to provide the proof of its source.

If you happen to win the lottery tomorrow, you will need to have that money for at least 90 days before it can be used for a down payment on a mortgage OR you need to get a letter from the lottery company for proof of proceeds and provide a transaction history to confirm the deposit.

 o Home Buyers Plan

- You were introduced to the New Home Buyers plan back in Chapter Four, which enables you to withdraw up to $25,000 from an RRSP plan tax-free to use as a down payment on a qualified property. The limit is per person and couples can each contribute for a combined maximum of $50,000. This program can be useful on its own or combined with other sources for your down payment.

  o Gifted

- A down payment can be gifted to you from anyone in your immediate family (Mother, Father, Grandparents, Aunts/Uncles, Siblings). You must include a gift letter signed by the family member which discloses the gift is not to be repaid. The gifted down payment may or may not need to clear the 90-day history. The size of the gift and the structure of the deal will determine how the gift is verified at the discretion of the lender.

  o Borrowed

- You can also use other credit facilities or loans to borrow your down payment. A personal loan, line-of-credit or any other credit sources may be used as your down payment. The government regulation will not permit a 100% financed mortgage and at least 5% cash must be put in. This can be stacked with a gifted down payment. If your plan includes using debt to finance your down payment, it must be included in your TDSR calculation.

  o Own Resources

- Of course, the old-fashioned way to provide a down payment is using your own cash. This cash may come from your bank account or you can also liquidate any other assets you might have. Just be sure that you can verify the source for at least 90 days prior to your mortgage funding. However, I always advise my clients that all documentation is best provided before the application is approved.

Income and Employment

Verifying income and employment can be simple and straightforward or it can be complicated and confusing depending on how you earn your income. The issue is not necessarily going to be how much you make, but rather, how confidently a lender can verify that income. Recall that one of the changes over the years is lenders are relying more on verifiable data than they are on character when reviewing creditworthiness. Income is one of those data points and can be a sensitive subject for many people. It's better to include how you will verify your income and employment as part of your plan and deal with the reality gap than to be caught in a downward spiral of frustration and unmet expectations.

<ins>Employment Income</ins>

If you receive a T4 for the income you've earned, you have employment income. At a minimum, you will need a letter of employment and a recent pay stub to verify your income, both dated within the last 30 days. You may be required to provide additional documentation if you are…

- A contract employee
- On permanent part-time
- On commission

Lenders associate additional risk when the source of income is variable, regardless of how much that income might be. They are only comfortable with the income they feel they can verify. A commissioned salesperson who makes $250,000 per year may have to provide more documentation than a salaried manager who makes $80,000.

Other types of documentation which may be required include, but are not limited to, two years Notice of Assessments (NOA), additional information on the letter of employment (e.g. hourly wage, guaranteed number of work hours), T4's and a copy of the employment contract.

Self-Employed

Verifying income and employment for self-employed individuals or business owners may be cumbersome. From a tax perspective, it might be in the best interests of the person to show as little income as possible in order to reduce the total taxes owed. This is counter productive when it comes to borrowing, because in this case it is better to show as much income as possible. This is a bit of a Catch 22 but is not impossible.

The T1 general is the start of the income verification for self-employed individuals or business owners. The T1 breaks down how you (or your accountant) calculated the taxable income. Lenders recognize there are many expenses deducted which would otherwise be paid personally, so they will add these expenses back into income. Examples include cell phones or deductions for utilities in a home office. Each case is unique but can certainly be managed when included in your plan.

Other Income

Other income may include dividends, interest income and capital gains, to name a few. If any of these sources need to be included for income verification, any type of documentation you can provide is useful. The lenders will be looking for reliability and consistency when it comes to other income (all income, for that matter).

If you made a substantial gain from selling a stock, the windfall might provide a good down payment but won't verify income for purposes of a mortgage. A dividend statement from a blue chip stock regularly paid over the last eight years would provide good verification.

The key points for income and employment as part of your plan are:

- o Income must be sufficient to meet TDSR requirements for the mortgage application amount.
- o Income must be verified to the satisfaction of the lender.

All of these details form part of the general conditions part of your plan. The more you understand what lenders are looking for and why, the better your plan will be

Qualifying Criteria (5C's)

If the down payment and income/employment verification is your responsibility within your plan, the *5C's of Credit* are the lender's contribution to your plan. While you have little control over the qualifying criteria of the lenders, your involvement is not completely passive. Your role in the *5C's* is to provide your professional mortgage advisor or broker with all the information possible to enable them to present a strong case to the lenders.

If you have a spotty credit history, provide them with a thorough explanation as to what happened in your life to cause those issues and what you have done to recover. Provide information on gaps in your employment history and future plans. Perhaps you have a complicated income source. Authorize your mortgage advisor to speak with your lawyers, accountants, bookkeeper or employer. Their job is to represent you. Your plan should help them present your best, most creditworthy you.

"You once borrowed a quarter from me in
grade school, and you never paid it back!"

The 5 C's of Credit

<u>Capacity</u>

Capacity is a measure of your ability to pay. The question lenders want to answer is, "Can you afford the payment?" The two debt service measures used are:

Gross Debt Service Ratio (GDSR) - I defined GDSR a little earlier as the ratio of total annual payment obligations divided by the gross annual income expressed as a percentage (%). The limit on GDSR is 39%, though the target GDSR is 35%.

$$GDSR = \frac{Principal + Interest + Taxes + Heat + [condo\ fees\ excluding\ heat]}{Gross\ Annual\ Income}$$

Total Debt Service Ratio (TDSR) - Includes the GDSR plus all other monthly payments, such as car payments, credit cards or other personal loans. The absolute max is 44%, though a good comfort level from a lender's risk perspective is 40%. The estimate used for credit cards is a minimum payment of 3% per month of the current balance. Depending on the lender, they may use 3% of the credit limit regardless of the balance. The logic is that you have access to the credit, and lenders want to evaluate your mortgage application for the worst-case scenario.

$$TDSR = \frac{GDSR + \text{All other debt obligations}}{\text{Gross Annual Income}}$$

SPECIAL NOTE: A particular lender may claw back on GDSR or TDSR if there are credit concerns. Just because they are willing to go up to 39% or 44% respectively doesn't mean the do for every file. Capacity is an indicator of where is their risk and they will decide a mortgage application accordingly. There are also B-lenders or alternatives who will accept higher debt service ratios and may go as high as 45-50% but this comes with a trade-off in the form of a lender fee between 1-3% and higher interest rates.

Capacity is an important piece of the credit approval process and its main driver is income and employment. Can you see why your plan is key and do you understand the importance of proper income verification?

Character

Character is a subjective measure indicating what kind of person you are. To a person who is trying to figure out who you are by looking at a computer screen of data, character plays a small role in the qualifying criteria. As I mentioned, it is contributing less and less as lenders rely more on hard data to evaluate applications. There is still a small role to be played here.

Reliability, stability, loyalty, and trust are all attributes a credit underwriter is trying to determine from your character. What types of characteristics do you think speak to your character?

○ Tenure at your job. Have you been with the same company for a length of time?

- ○ Position at your job. Do you hold a level of authority (manager, executive)?
- ○ How long have you lived at your current residence?
- ○ Do you move often?
- ○ Have you made amends if you've had credit challenges in the past?
- ○ What is your track record for accumulating assets?
- ○ What is your total net worth picture?

These are all questions an underwriter is trying answer about you. When you include this in your plan, you can make the underwriter's job easier to approve your mortgage application.

Collateral

Collateral is the asset being used as security on the debt. In a mortgage, the collateral is the property. The lender approves the home you are buying in addition to your credit. One of the key factors in approving the collateral is LTV.

History of the property also plays a part. Here are three real-life examples I have encountered where the history of the property had an impact on the assessed value of the home:

Tales From The Field

Preserved wood foundation.
The property had a preserved wood foundation and there were only a handful of lenders or insurers who would mortgage this property. The limited access to lenders/insurers meant that the buyers had limited choices for a mortgage.

Former Grow-Op
Homes that were used as growing operations for marijuana can be near impossible to find a lender to write a mortgage for; even if the property has proof of remediation.

Potential Re-assessment
Another issue that can affect a mortgage when it comes to collateral is Re-assessment. The assessed value of the home is used to calculate property taxes in municipalities. Both lenders and insurers want to stay away from properties that are to be potentially re-assessed.

Now we come full circle from the discussion about past housing prices and trend analysis. All these pieces are considered in the collateral approval.

Capital

The capital requirement is part of your net worth and is evaluated in a couple of ways. The first is how much of a down payment you are willing to put in. The down payment does more than reduce risk of debt for the lender. It's also a signal of your financial commitment to buy your own home. The larger the down payment, the stronger the message.

Your other forms of capital are also reviewed. This includes and investments into stocks, bonds, mutual funds, segregated funds, cash-value insurance policies, hard assets (artwork, investment grade diamonds, etc.). When an underwriter reviews the capital in your net worth statement, they are reviewing how much money is tied up in these line items as well as how liquid they are. In other words, how quickly can you convert them to cash if you needed to work your way out of a cash flow crunch. For example, if you own stocks and bonds in a brokerage account, you can probably liquidate the portfolio and get the cash within a few days. A rare piece of artwork is not nearly as liquid, regardless of how much value it holds.

Clearly, the more capital you have, the stronger your credit application will be.

Credit

Your credit history is the most critical piece of your qualifying criteria. You credit report represents how you have actually handled your affairs in the past. What does your payment history look like? No item is minor on your credit report and every little piece tells a story. There are two major credit reports used in Canada--Equifax Canada and TransUnion Canada. Most lenders will use one more than the other and there is no logic to which one they choose.

The major sections of your credit report include:

- o Contact/Employment Information and Credit Score
- o List of Credit Inquiries
- o Public Records
- o Trade Accounts

The contact/employment information and credit score serve two purposes:

- Verifies that your address and employment information on your credit application match your credit report.
- Provides your credit score.

```
[3] File Requested by: JDOE
Identification
Name:                TEST, FILE, EQUIFAX
Current Address:     5650 YONGE STREET, TORONTO, ON, M2M 4G3
Previous Address:    110, SHEPPARD AVE EAST, TORONTO, ON, M2B 6S1

Date of Birth: CCYY/MM/DD,
SIN: 999-999-999
Reference:           JDOE

Employment
Employer, Occupation: TESTS MECHANIC SHOP, OWNER

[4] Subject 1: Alert, Score, Identification, Inquiries, Employment, Summary, Public
Records, Banking, Consumer Statement or Alert.

Consumer Alert
[5] Warnings
Invalid Social Insurance Number

[6] SAFESCAN
SF-0 Possible True Name Fraud

[7] Product Score
Equifax Risk Score          609
Serious delinquency and public record or collection filed
Time since delinquency is too recent or unknown
Number of accounts with delinquency
Medium Risk Region, Subprime Credit File

Bankruptcy Navigator Index   230
Age of derogatory public records
Average age of retail trades
Number of recent inquiries

Identification

[8] Unique Number 1234567899
[9] File Number 00-00000000-00-000
[10] Date File Opened: CCYY/MM/DD
[11] Date of Last Activity: CCYY/MM/DD
[12] DOB: CCYY/MM/DD
[13] SIN: 999-999-999
[13B] ** Consumer Statement **
[14] Name:                TEST, FILE, EQUIFAX
[15] Current Address:     5650 YONGE STREET, TORONTO, ON, M2M 4G3
[16] Since:               CCYY/MM
[17] Reported:            STS Reported
[18] Former Address:      110, SHEPPARD, TORONTO, ON, M2B 6S1
Since:                    CCYY/MM
Reported:                 Tape Reported
[19] 2nd Former Address:  2314, 11 TH AVE 1201, TORONTO, ON, M4W 3C1
Since:                    CCYY/MM
Reported:                 Tape Reported
[20] AKA/Also Known As:   PRETEND, FILE, EQUIFAX

Telephone #
[21] Telephone #: 555-555-1234 EXTN: Residential/Home
Date first reported: CCYY/MM/DD
Date last received: CCYY/MM/DD
```

The credit inquiries are the next section of your report. Every time you apply for credit, the inquiry and its date are listed on your report. That means every time you filled out a credit card application to get the free gift while walking through a shopping mall shows up as an inquiry, regardless if you were approved or not. The number and span of credit inquiries are important because too many inquiries over an extended period of time will bring your credit score down. Additionally, having lots of inquiries makes it look like you may be shopping for credit. People who frequently shop for credit often have difficulty managing their credit. They often use credit to finance a lifestyle they cannot afford. This shows up most often with consumer debt.

Clearly, you will be expected to shop when making major purchases like a home or a car. Inquiries, for sake of the credit score and analysis, that are similar in nature in a very short time period are grouped together and are considered one inquiry.

Inquiries
[22] Subject shows 3 inquires since CCYY/MM/DD
[23] Member Inquiries:

Date	Member Name	Telephone
CCYY/MM/DD	ABC BANK	222-555-3333
CCYY/MM/DD	RETAIL WORLD	555-555-1234
CCYY/MM/DD	CANADA CAR LOANS	555-999-0000
CCYY/MM/DD	MORTGAGE WORLD	000-555-0987

[24] Total number of inquiries: 28
[25] Foreign Bureau Inquiries:

Date	Member	Description
CCYY/MM/DD	ABC CREDIT	372DC00000

Public records are a list of collections, judgments, consumer proposals and bankruptcies. Any items listed in this category are bad for your credit score and will raise questions with the underwriters. The information an underwriter can find is the date of the record, the amount, who registered the record and a description.

The only thing you can do with this information is to make sure you provide a thorough explanation of what happened and why. There is no avoiding it, and at times it may feel uncomfortable. It will come out no matter what. When you are working with true professionals, there is no judgment. The truth is, there is very little that an experienced mortgage advisor or underwriter hasn't seen or heard.

The trade accounts form the core of your credit report. The trade lines are every piece of credit you have had over the past seven years along with the details and 24-36-month payment history. The key elements on your trade accounts are:

- Name of lender and contact information
- High Credit
- Current Balance
- Payment Status
- Payment History
- Date Opened
- Date Last Reported
- Type of account

Your trade lines have two components--the type of trade line and the payment status.

There are several account types which indicate what type of trade line is reporting on your credit report:

I - Installment loan
R - Revolving credit
O - Mobile Phone
BB -Mortgages

The numbers signify the payment status of the credit:

1 - Current
2 - 30 days in arrears
3 - 60 days in arrears
4 - 90 days in arrears
5 - 120 days in arrears
6 - 180 days in arrears
7 - Orderly Payment of Debts (OPD or Consumer Proposal
8 - Repossession
9 - Balance written off

Numbers 5 and 6, which indicate an account is over 120 days in arrears, are rarely seen on a credit report because the account is usually closed due to write-off by that point. Few lenders will carry debts or other obligations much longer than 90 days, though each have their own policies.

The accounts on your credit report either report as an installment loan (I, revolving (R, mobile phone (O or mortgage (BB and are paired with a number 1-9.

An 'I1' is an installment loan that is current. An 'R9' is a revolving credit (like a credit card which has been written off to bad debt. All of these trade lines tell the story of how you handle your affairs. As I mentioned before, every piece tells part of the story.

Brett Roessel

Your credit is *YOUR FINANCIAL REPUTATION*. It is difficult to build, easy to damage and hard to repair. Make sure you take care of your credit as best as you can.

Here's what the lenders are looking for:

○ Good payment history
○ Comparable sized high credit - though many may not have had any credit the size of a mortgage.
○ Length of time trades reporting - minimum two years
○ Utilization of credit - 50% or less of available credit being used.
○ Number and frequency of credit inquiries.

The qualifying criteria provides most of the narrative about your creditworthiness and forms a substantial part of your plan. How well you and your advisor plan will determine how quickly you can get to your ultimate goal--a mortgage approval. The more complete you can make your plan along with your advisor, the sooner you can get out to shopping for your new home and the more certainty you may have that you will qualify to finance it.

Step 4 - **Prepayment Privileges**

The fourth and final piece of your plan and *buying the garage before the car* is identifying what types of prepayment privileges you will need. Prepayments can be a powerful tool to save interest and as a source of a contingency fund when times get tough. Every lender has some variation of prepayment options, though the terms will vary from lender to lender.

A prepayment privilege is a payment directly to principal without an interest penalty. You will read more about payout penalties in Chapter Seven. Prepayments are most often permitted in 10%, 15% or 20% of the original mortgage amount. Most lenders have a prepayment option of 10% every calendar year. For example, if your mortgage originated at $500,000, you could make any number of principal payments for up to $50,000 during the calendar year. The next year is reset and you can do it all over again.

You have already seen the power of compounding. How much of a saving benefit do you think you would have if you were to start making lump sum payments on your mortgage every year? The savings would be massive. Prepayment privileges are often expressed as 10+10 or 20+20. The first number indicates how much of your mortgage principal you can pay down every calendar year without penalty. The second number means you can increase your mortgage payment by that amount and apply it directly to principal. A 10+10 means you can prepay 10% every calendar year and increase your mortgage payment by 10%. Some lenders will permit a lump sum AND a payment increase while others will lump the payments into one cumulative total.

There are other prepayment privileges available as well:

Match a Payment

The *match a payment is* exactly as it sounds. This option enables you to match a mortgage payment and put towards principal. When you match a payment, it will reduce your mortgage schedule and have you paid out one period sooner (week, month, etc.).

Miss a Payment

This option also means exactly the way it sounds. The *miss a payment* option is the exact opposite of the *match a payment.* You can skip a mortgage payment when you have prepaid a corresponding match payment. This will extend your mortgage schedule, but only as far as your original amortization schedule.

All of these options have practical solutions for many different people. Commission salespeople who regularly come into large sums of money at one time can choose to prepay parts of their mortgage. Seasonal workers can choose to match a payment for the months they are working and then miss a payment for the months they are off.

The prepayment privileges are the last part of your plan and should be discussed with your professional mortgage advisor or broker.

Buying the garage before the car will set you up for a great start to your homebuying journey. Purchasing your Big Asset doesn't have to be scary or complicated. It only takes a little bit of effort on the front end with a good plan. There is no need to be frustrated through the process, as long as you recognize the reality gap and work to overcome it.

Ideas to Remember

○   Buy the garage before the car. It would be a shame to lose the home you wanted for the car you don't really need.

○   Manage the reality gap with a good plan.

○   Developing a plan is the order of operations in your buying journey.

○   A good plan has four distinct steps to map out.

○   These general conditions will fill the majority of your plan--down payment, income/employment, qualifying criteria

○   Prepayment privileges is the fourth step of your plan and can buy you flexibility or substantial interest savings.

CHAPTER SIX
INSURE OR NOT TO INSURE???

*"Getting straight with your money is as complicated as a
trip to the grocery store: You need a comparison shop,
add and subtract, stick with a plan, and ask questions -
nothing more."*

~ Elizabeth Warren

Insurance can be a sensitive subject for some and an absolute no-brainer for others. When it comes to your Big Asset, there is insurance you may not have any choice but to take, discretionary insurances most agree would be a good idea to have and then other insurances you may gladly pay for and hope never to use.

With respect to your mortgage, the decision to insure or not to insure begins with the down payment. You've briefly read about default insurance in previous chapters and I will provide a more detailed explanation about what it entails. But default insurance is not the only protection available. If you are going to spend hundreds of thousands of dollars (or perhaps millions) and a substantial portion of your life and income, would you at the very least want to know your options for protecting your biggest asset?

That's what this chapter is about. My wish for you in this chapter, as it has been throughout this book, is to give you enough information to put you in a position to make good decisions. In my opinion, insurance is one of the least understood financial instruments, misunderstood in the way most people are unaware of what the real purpose of insurance is. Many know how it works. Premiums are paid, and if a certain event happens, the insurance company pays for it. To most people, I think it comes across as a form of gambling. The insured is betting something will happen, and the insurer is betting it won't. That might be part of its function, but it's certainly not the purpose. That's what casinos are for.

My perspective of insurance is to protect our two most important assets--our time and our ability to earn income. You probably thought I was going to say our home is one of our most important assets, especially considering the topic of this book. The time we have and our ability to earn income are our most important assets. Without either, there is no home. The ultimate benefit of insurance to protect our loss of time and ability to earn income.

Default Insurance

After all that talk about insurance protecting your time and ability to earn income, we're going to start this section talking about default insurance, which protects the lender. Default insurance protects the lender in the case the borrower defaults on the mortgage. Mortgage default insurance is required on all mortgages with down payments of less than 20%, which are known as high-ratio mortgages.

Why on earth would you want to pay for insurance that protects the lender instead of you? You would for a couple of reasons. The first is you can opt out of default insurance if you have at least a 20% down payment. If you have less than the 20%, your only other choice is to wait and continue to save for more of a down payment. Depending on your situation, there is a high cost of waiting, as you have already read about. The second reason is a lender may provide incentives such as lower rates for opting into default insurance, which can then offset part of the premium.

SPECIAL NOTE: Default insurance is not to be confused with mortgage insurance (creditor insurance). Default insurance pays the creditor if you default on the mortgage and the lender forecloses. Mortgage insurance is a product you purchase which pays the balance of your mortgage if you pass away. More on that later in this chapter.

Who Provides Default Insurance?

There are three organizations in Canada who provide default insurance:

- ○ Canadian Mortgage Housing Corporation (Crown Corporation owned by Federal Government)
- ○ Genworth Canada
- ○ Canada Guaranty

There are very subtle differences between the three providers who generally have the same rate premiums. The premium rates are posted publicly on their respective websites and are updated periodically. The biggest difference between these providers are in the special programs they offer. For example, CMHC will lend up to $40,000 for purchase plus improvements, while the other two will insure up to 10%.

The choice of provider is yours to make. The decision of which provider is a better fit for your default insurance will come from your plan discussed in the last chapter. This is also why having a trusted professional mortgage advisor is a must-have, to help you navigate these pathways they travel down every day while it is likely a single occurrence for you.

What else do I need to know?

Your choice of insurer will depend on any special programs to which you need access, as well as the relationship the lender has with that insurer. As is the case with many businesses across several industries, businesses who have good relationships with each other grant some latitude. The mortgage industry isn't any different in that respect. Some lenders have a better relationship with a particular insurer and other lenders have a good relationship with a different insurer. Though the choice of insurer is yours, the best choice will likely be the one who has the better relationship with your lender.

There are two ways to pay the premium for the default insurance:

- o Pay it as a lump sum out of pocket.
- o Add it to your mortgage.

You will need the cash to pay the premium out-of-pocket, which could affect your down payment, depending on your personal financial situation. The alternative is to add the cost of the premium to your mortgage, which will have a negligible affect on your payment--but you will be paying interest on the insurance premium.

Title Insurance

Title insurance is a lesser known form of protection when it comes to your Big Asset. The title insurance is a policy you can buy to protect you from any issues that exist with the property at the time of your purchase which you may not know about. Some lenders require you to purchase title insurance as part of their conditions for approval. This is more commonly known as Creditor Title Insurance. It is HIGHLY recommended that you purchase Homeowner Title Insurance at the same time because of significant cost savings.

Title Issues - title defects, encumbrances, liens
Off-Title Issues - lack of legal access, zoning non-compliance, lack of building permits, incorrect search queries
Transactional Issues - title fraud, survey issues
Duty to Defend - covers legal costs incurred to defend your interests in the property

What are the use cases for title insurance?

There are many ways title insurance would protect you. Here are a couple of use cases and how title insurance have helped these homeowners...

1. Lack of a building permit

Problem: A couple purchased a new home with the intention of renovating the main floor. When they inquired with their local municipality about removing a wall on the main floor, they were advised it would depend on the structural strength of the basement. The homeowners advised the municipality that they were unable to confirm the structural integrity of the basement because it was finished with drywall. This revealed that the previous owners had finished the basement without the required building permits from the municipality. The municipality mandated that the homeowners obtain a building permit for the work done in the basement, which required they first bring the basement up to building code requirements - additional renovations they had not budgeted for which added up to $46,303.19.

Solution: Fortunately, they had a homeowner title insurance policy from one of the title insurers which covered against this type of loss. We provided a settlement payment to cover the full amount of their loss and the homeowners were able to proceed with their open-concept renovations as planned.

2. Tax and utility arrears

Problem: Shortly after moving in, a couple received a notice from the city regarding outstanding tax and water utility charges amounting to $2,034.79. This was a very unwelcome surprise given their tight budget as first-time homebuyers.

Solution: Because of their title insurance coverage, they were spared the over $2,000.00 expense when the claim was paid out by the title insurer.

3. Work ordersProblem: Just before closing, a seller received notice of an outstanding work order which was in existence prior to their purchase of the property. The cost of the work required to lift the order was $11,315.00 and the prospective purchaser was ready to walk away from the deal, not wanting the expense or the hassle.

Solution: Not only did the title insurer pay the $11,315.00 on behalf of the vendor to resolve the work order, but also issued a free policy to the new purchaser and worked with them to resolve the issues in question. The deal went ahead as planned, closing on time to the satisfaction of all involved parties.

4. Fraud

Problem: A purchaser with an investment property received notice stating the mortgage was in default and the lender would be taking possession of the property. The insured sought counsel, as he knew his mortgage was in good standing. An investigation revealed the title was fraudulently transferred from the insured homeowner and a mortgage in the amount of $165,000 had been fraudulently registered on the title. Mortgage funds were paid to the fraudulent transferee, who was now nowhere to be found.

Solution: The title insurer co-ordinated and retained counsel on his behalf and ultimately paid out $12,548.09 in legal fees to remove the mortgage from that title and rightfully transfer the title back to him.

Who provides title insurance?

The two main providers of title insurance in Canada include First Canadian Title and FNF Canada. The premium is a one-time fee out of pocket and can be purchased at any time. The coverage is for the life of home ownership and the average premium is under $500.

When you read through the use cases, do you see how having this information can be valuable? The decision to insure or not to insure will always be yours but lack of education will never be a reason going forward from today.

Home Insurance

Home insurance is a pretty common subject so I will briefly touch on it here. Default insurance protects the lender, title insurance protects you as a buyer and the lender (depending on the type of policy purchased) while home insurance protects your Big Asset. Your lender will require a minimum amount of home insurance which is also in your best interest to carry, similar to the way auto insurance is a requirement but is also in the best interest of the vehicle owner. Insurance is one of those products we buy and hope never to have to use it but are glad we have it when we need it.

Lender Required Insurance

Lenders will take every step necessary to reduce their risk, and that includes the collateral on the mortgage. Your lender will require you to carry fire protection and replacement insurance on your home. This is a moment where the lender's interests and yours are aligned. Even though these insurances are required by the lender, they are also in your best interest to protect your Big Asset.

Other Property Insurance

Flood Insurance - water may come from different sources to ruin your flooring, furniture and even the foundation. Water may come from a sewer back up, ground water and overland.

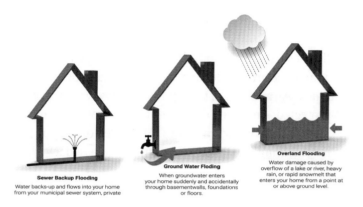

Sewer Backup Flooding
Water backs-up and flows into your home
from your municipal sewer system, private

Ground Water Floding
When groundwater enters
your home suddenly and accidentally
through basementwalls, foundations
or floors.

Overland Flooding
Water damage caused by
overflow of a lake or river, heavy
rain, or rapid snowmelt that
enters your home from a point at
or above ground level.

Theft Insurance - Protects against the loss of any of your belongings and any damages to your home from the result of a break-in.

As with all insurance coverage, you need to decide what is right for you with the help of a licensed insurance professional.

Protection Insurance

We have not yet discussed protecting your two most important assets--time and your ability to earn an income. That is exactly what protection insurance is for. Protection insurance is for you. These are tools and strategies you can use to protect your income if you get hurt, sick or pass away. Sadly enough, so few people spend much time thinking about protecting where their income comes from. It seems to me most spend more time planning their vacations than they do their financial futures.

If that happens to be you, good news, because that ends right now as you continue on to read the rest of this book.

Protecting Against Loss of Time

For some, this may feel like a morbid topic. Imagining what would happen if we died is an uncomfortable discussion and many people are uneasy with the subject. An analysis of the top 1% wealthy would reveal they are very well-protected. And so are their families. What would happen to your family if you were no longer with them? How well off do you think they would be if something happened to you and you passed away, and your income along with you?

Just looking back at the stats from Chapter Two, most people can't go without one paycheque, never mind if at least half of their monthly income was wiped out. You are in a position to make a sound financial decision about protecting yourself. There are two ways to do so with respect to your Big Asset:

1. Mortgage Insurance
Mortgage insurance is a vehicle which is widely known and publicly discussed. Mortgage insurance is a monthly premium paid to cover the mortgage if you were to die. The challenge with mortgage insurance is that it protects the creditor more than it does your family. It's not an accident that it is often referred to as creditor insurance.

This insurance is a level premium with declining coverage. Its function is that upon approval of a claim, the insurer pays the lender for the balance of the mortgage and the home is paid in full. While it is a nice feature, it doesn't help your family put food on the table or boots on their feet without the income you were bringing in. There are other products which might serve your financial needs a little better.

2. Life Insurance

Term or permanent life insurance is a welcome alternative to mortgage insurance. Its function is your monthly premium pays for a level face value. The death benefit will never change and cannot be taken away as long as the premiums are paid on time. This type of insurance requires medical underwriting and not everyone will qualify.

How do these compare with respect to my mortgage? Suppose your mortgage was $500,000 over 30 years. As time passes and you are making your mortgage payments, the principal balance is reduced. The amount of premium you pay for both insurances stay level (top line). Assume you passed away in year six and the balance of your mortgage was $400,000. If you were in a mortgage insurance policy, only the balance of the mortgage at $400,000 would be paid directly to the lender and the home would be paid off.

If you were protected by a life insurance policy, the face value of $500,000 would be paid to your beneficiary. They could then choose to pay part, all or none of the mortgage, keeping the difference in cash. The cash might come in useful as your family adjusts to their new living circumstances.

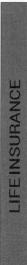
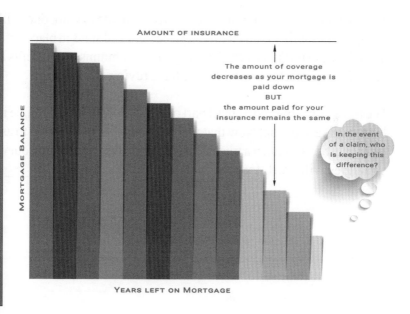

Both insurance products have a purpose and their limitations. That's why I feel blessed to have all the different industry partners I do. I am able to help my clients by putting them in touch with competent professionals who can help them make sound financial decisions on all sides.

Protecting Against Loss of Income

Protection of your income applies to if you get sick or hurt. These are known as living benefits and help fill in the gaps when you are temporarily unable to work because of some life event.

Critical Illness - Pays you a lump sum tax free when you are diagnosed with one or more of the covered conditions. Examples include certain types of cancers, a heart attack, a major organ transplant, strokes, and a host of other conditions.

Disability - Protects your income if you are unable to work due to illness or injury. Disability is an income replacement and stays in place until you are able to get back to work. The programs, premiums and benefits are as varied as the mortgage options we have reviewed so far.

We have only covered a small part of what protection insurance is and how it will affect you. Now that you have enough information to ask the right questions, contact a trusted insurance professional to find out which strategies will work for you.

Ideas to Remember

o   Insurance is to protect your two most important assets--time and the ability to earn income.

o   Default insurance protects the lender.

o   Lender's requirement for default insurance is dependent on the size of your down payment.

o   Title insurance protects you from previous owners.

o   Home or property insurance protects your Big Asset and all of your belongings.

o   Protection insurance is for you.

o   Mortgage insurance is creditor insurance that pays out the balance of your mortgage when you pass away.

o   Life insurance pays out a tax-free death benefit to your beneficiary, who chooses what they need to do with the cash.

o   Critical illness and disability protect you if you are unable to work because of sickness or injury.

CHAPTER SEVEN
RATES—FIXED VERSUS VARIABLE

"There is something permanent,
and something extremely profound in owning a home."

~ Kenny Guinn

What do you think about this statement: *The type of rate you choose depends more on the type of person you are than it does the size of the number.* In this cost-conscious industry, it even sounds strange to say it. How does personality even matter when shopping for a mortgage rate?

It matters a lot.

The two types of rates are fixed and variable. Both have their own characteristics and affect the borrower in different ways. What type of borrower are you?

- Do you like structure and reliable/consistent payments?
- Are you comfortable with a fluctuation in your payments?

Your tolerance for variability is a better indicator of the type of rate you should pursue. I have met quite a few clients in my career who shop for the lowest possible rate to the lowest payment. I still see this mistake all the time. I have found borrowers who are rate shopping are not necessarily looking for value. It's a signal to me that they haven't completed their plan as you read about in Chapter Five. They didn't follow the order of operations I laid out and have left out some of the key steps. Instead of managing the reality gap, they are frustrated with unmet expectations.

When rate shopping becomes about trying to get the lowest payment, they are setting themselves up for failure. Quite often, the lowest possible rate comes with some variability. There have been rate increases four times in the last year and a half. My question is: *Will this buyer be able to absorb one or more of these rate increases if they absolutely need the lowest payment?*

The mortgage structure needs to be centered on the strategy and not the rate or its type. There is a large knowledge gap about fixed versus variable rates among borrowers. Many are exposing themselves to payment shock when there is fluctuation. It requires just a little bit of knowledge of how rates are calculated and what factors cause them to change.

For instance, the fixed rate is determined by pricing in the bond market (10, 20, and 30-year bonds while variable rates correlate with the prime lending rate. In either case, both are affected by the economy at the time. GDP, labour expectations, forecasts, and other economic events which have an influence. None of which matter if borrowers lack the basic understanding and the ability to apply the knowledge.

The result is either a mortgage by default or by design. One will always have to react to the events and will never be able to live comfortably with the outcome. The other has applied some simple lessons and designed their mortgage in a way which provides the most amount of value and flexibility.

For the rest of the chapter, I will give you as much detail as we can reasonably fit in with respect to mortgage rates and how they will impact you.

Fixed Rates

The fixed-rate mortgage is exactly the way it sounds. The interest rate stays the same throughout the period. Since the interest never changes, the payments will also stay fixed. Even though the payments stay the same throughout the term, the mix of principal and interest still follows the amortization schedule.

Recall the chart from Chapter Four:

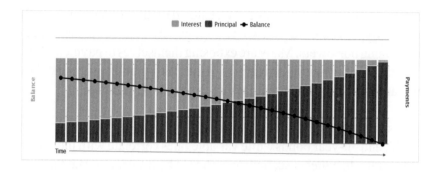

This chart demonstrates what a fixed-rate mortgage would look like. You see that the payment across the top remains constant. The principal and interest follow the amortization schedule as expected. This mortgage structure works well for people who like the predictability of their payments. They can rely on the consistency of payments and know exactly what is going to happen with their mortgage month after month throughout the mortgage period. The payment and the rate stay the same regardless of what is happening with the outside world. The economy can change and so can the markets. The fixed rate will not change until the mortgage comes up for renewal.

There are Trade Offs...

The first trade off is the fixed rate is typically set higher than the prime rate. For a period of time, you may be paying a higher rate than is available to you. You would be trading interest savings for convenience and certainty. The good news is that the mortgage is less about the lowest rate and more about the value of the structure.

Next, fixed-rate mortgages (closed) have a higher payout penalty for early exit. The payout costs are the greater of either.

- o 3 months of interest
- o Interest Rate Differential (IRD)

As a rule of thumb, if you are within a year left on your term, your payout penalty will most likely be the three months of interest. Alternatively, if you have longer than one year left on your term, IRD will most likely be your payout penalty. This isn't true every time, but it is a good place to start for understanding.

Original Mortgage	$500,000
Original Term	5 yrs
Current Balance	$300,000
Balance of Term	3 yrs
Fixed Mortgage Rate	4%
Posted Rate	3%

Calculating Three Months of Interest

Current Balance x Fixed Mortgage Rate/4

*= $300,000 x 4% / 4 = **$3000***

Calculating IRD

(Fixed Mortgage Rate – Posted Rate [Closest Rate to Remaining Term] x Current Balance x Balance of Term

= (4% - 3% x $300,000 x 3 = **$9000**

This is why your plan is so important. If part of your plan is an early exit, you need to factor the payout penalties as part of your decision. The $6000 difference in payout penalty is significant and it is important for you to weigh in all of the trade-offs of a fixed-rate mortgage.

How Fixed Rate is Determined...

Fixed-rate mortgage loans are primarily influenced by the yield on Canadian government bonds (bond yields) of corresponding maturity. Refer to the chart below and you will notice that there is a near perfect correlation between the five-year fixed rate and the corresponding Canadian government bond.

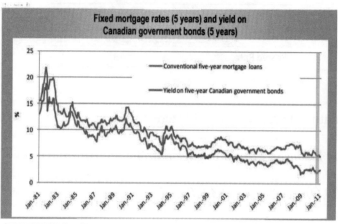

Source: Statistics Canada

You might be a fixed-rate mortgage person if you like the stability and certainty of your payment. You are okay paying a little higher interest rate and plan to stay in your home for a long period of time.

Variable Rates

Variable mortgage rates are essentially determined by commercial banks' prime rates, which are mainly influenced by the Bank of Canada's key interest rate. Thus, an increase in the key interest rate almost automatically leads to an equivalent increase in variable mortgage rates. The Bank of Canada raises its key interest rate when it wants to fight inflation.

Variable rates have historically been lower than the five-year posted rate. There was a brief period when the discounted fixed rates were close to the variable rates, but that was an anomaly and unusual.

You will usually see the variable rates posted as a discount or premium on the lender's prime rate. For example, you might see it as prime +0.5% or prime -0.25%. The base rate with the lenders is tied to the Bank of Canada prime rate. Generally, when the Bank of Canada raises its rates, the lenders will raise theirs.

Refer back to the fixed mortgage chart. If I were to draw a variable rate mortgage chart on the same axis, the principal payment and the balance would look exactly the same. The only change would be in the interest portion. With variable rate mortgage, the interest portion and the total payment would rise when the base rate increased. On the other hand, as the base rate decreased, the interest portion and the total payment would sink. As you can envision, the only factor which changes with the variable-rate mortgage is the interest. The amortization period doesn't change and neither does the schedule of principal payments.

How Variable Rate is Determined...

The bank's economists will monitor a number of factors, including GDP, Unemployment and the Bank of Canada Prime Rate. Although the prime rate is usually a trigger for banks to raise or lower their base rate, the lenders are not obligated to do either. Most times they do. There have been periods when the Bank of Canada lowered their prime rate and the lenders did not follow suit, by keeping their base rate the same.

These fluctuations can change as often as the government chooses and there is no cap on the rate. Mortgages signed to a variable rate have no rate protection. In theory, the variable rate could skyrocket and drive the mortgage payment up. That is quite unlikely, but it is possible.

Build a Good Strategy and Plan

Fixed rate is not necessarily better than a variable rate and vice versa. The important piece is which rate strategy will work best within your plan and reflect the type of borrower you are. The variable rate mortgage comes with some variability and some risk. The reward for dealing with the uncertainty is the lower interest costs associated with the rate type.

However, a good plan and strategy can earn the best of both worlds. What if you wanted some payment certainty AND wanted to take advantage of interest savings, flexibility and lower payout penalties associated with variable rate mortgages? One strategy would be to implement one or more of the prepayment privileges and structure a fixed payment schedule with a variable rate. For instance, if your monthly mortgage payment was $1100 and was based on a variable rate of base + 0.25, you could use the 10% payment increase privilege without penalty and create a fixed payment of $1210. As the interest rate starts to climb, the increased payment absorbs the interest increase. As the interest rate falls, more of your payment goes toward principal.

We come full circle to Chapter Five and the value of your plan. If you identify that these are some of your priorities, these strategies may be set up and you can take comfort that you are somewhat protected. You're still at risk of no cap on the variable rate, but you will be in a much better position to manage it. Your advisor will be able to calculate at what rate your payment will change and put together a plan of what you will do if that happens so you can avoid any payment shock. Talk about managing the reality gap!

As is the common theme throughout this book, there isn't one strategy that is right or wrong. The only thing that matters is what is right for you.

Open versus Closed Terms

The final variable in selecting your mortgage strategy to buy your home is the term. Your mortgage options are a Fixed or Variable rate combined with Open or Closed terms.

Open Terms

In an open mortgage, repayment terms are more flexible than a closed mortgage, which does not usually allow for prepayment without penalty.

Sound too good to be true? I am sure you've figured out by now that you will always be paying for value. An open-term mortgage comes with flexibility which affords you options. As a result, open-term rates (fixed or variable) are usually a little higher than the closed-term rates.

An open term mortgage might be a good fit for you if you have a short-term exit strategy. That is to say, if you are going to want to pay out the mortgage because you have a lump sum you can put down or you plan to sell the house before the term comes due. An open-term mortgage may make sense because the additional interest will save the payout penalty, which can be costly.

Closed Terms

Closed mortgages have a prepayment limit, which means you are only permitted to pay 10%,15% or 20% of the original principal balance of the mortgage per calendar year. The closed mortgage also comes attached with a payout penalty of the greater of three months of interest or an interest rate differential. As you read in the payout examples earlier in the book, these penalties may cost many thousands of dollars. The exit will require planning and strategy to deal with the penalties.

Closed terms are most attractive when you know you will be carrying the mortgage to term and would like to take advantage of a lower interest rate.

Once more, neither option is better than the other. The only thing that matters is if one or the other is right for you.

I have only given you an overview and could probably write a whole new book on the details of each topic regarding rates and terms. To this point, you definitely have enough education that you can meet with a licensed mortgage advisor and put together a solid plan to buy your Big Asset. You probably even got to know yourself a little bit better. Did you get a glimpse of where your comfort zone is? It's only when we start to push the boundaries of our comfort zones that they start to expand.

Writing this book reminds me of the first time a I learned a magic trick. At first glance, the magic seemed impossible. Once I had an expert who knew how to competently perform the trick show me how to do it, it appeared basic and simple--only after I learned. All of your mortgage options and strategies appear to be an impossible trick until an expert teaches you how they're done.

Ideas to Remember

○ Choosing the right rate option is less about chasing the lowest possible rate and more about getting the most value out of your mortgage.

○ Fixed rates trade off a higher interest rate in exchange for payment stability and certainty.

○ The benchmark for fixed rates is the equivalent term on Canadian government bonds.

○ You may be a fixed rate person if you enjoy a stable payment and are comfortable paying a higher interest rate.

○ Variable rates follow the Bank of Canada prime rate.

○ The variable-rate mortgage payment can fluctuate, and the payment will rise or fall with the lender's base rate.

○ Open terms can be prepaid at any time without penalty while Closed terms will have a payout penalty of three months or IRD.

CHAPTER EIGHT
HOME BUYING – FIRST TIME OR REPEAT

*"If I were asked to name the chief benefit of the house,
I should say: the house shelters daydreaming,
the house protects the dreamer,
the house allows one to dream in peace."*

~ Gaston Bachelard

You don't know what you don't know. You may be a first-time homebuyer and are excited about starting this new journey to find and finance your Big Asset. Perhaps you have bought your home and renewal is coming up. You may also be a seasoned veteran looking to buy your second or third property. Whatever your situation is, I can assure you the industry has already changed since the last time you mortgaged a home.

I recently helped a client because her mortgage renewal was coming due and we were considering switching lenders to get a better rate. Since the last time she'd written her mortgage, the lenders had changed their income requirements and were no longer accepting child tax credits as part of income verification. This varies from lender to lender. Thankfully, we were able to verify the income we needed without it and she could continue with her mortgage uninterrupted.

Nearly everything is in a state of constant flux. We have already seen how often the regulations can change from Chapter Four. We witnessed the birth and death of the 40-year term within the same decade. It wasn't that long ago we were able to refinance a mortgage for up to 95% LTV. That ratio is down to a max of 80% today. We were able to qualify HELOCS with an LTV of 80%, which is down to 65% today.

The Bank of Canada had not increased their rate in over eight years and then we see four increases in the matter of 1.5 years. The financial industry is in constant evolution. The rules keep changing and the economy continues to change. How can consumers possibly keep up to date?

The economy is a violent roller coaster. Oil prices experienced a steep decline affecting the entire economy. Now that there is somewhat of a recovery in world prices, our biggest industry fights to get competitive. Pipelines are being approved and then recanted. Foreign governments are attempting to rewrite trade agreements which have been in place for three decades. Then they impose substantial trade tariffs.

Technology is quickly reshaping the way the world does business. Financial technology (Fintech) companies are aggressively challenging the status quo. Every month there is a new service which can do something faster, cheaper, and better. They are starting to open up the world to give access to a world population without financial services. They are making it possible for complete strangers to lend each other money and do so profitably with minimal risk.

What will change next? What was normal five years ago is not normal today. In another five years we will be amid a new normal. What has changed in your life?

You are not the same person today you were five years ago and will be a different person in another five years. Have you unloaded an old relationship or starting a new one? Have you changed your job or even found a new career? Perhaps you started your family, or you added a couple of new family members.

Whether you are a first-time homebuyer or a repeat purchaser, little has stayed the same. Whatever you knew before has now changed. There is a lot to know and even more to learn.

Credit: The Most Important of the 5C's

I touched on the *5C's* of credit in Chapter Five. Lenders have used the *5C's* as a core part of the underwriting process to decision credit applications for as long as I can remember.

Capacity | *Character* | *Collateral* | *Capital* | ***Credit***

Your ability to pay, your willingness to pay, what you can provide in case you don't pay, what you have before you can't afford to pay anymore and how you have paid in the past are the questions the *5C's* are designed to answer. This is an effort to predict your financial future, the likelihood the lender might get hurt and how badly. This another way to ask, "What is the risk?"

The value of each of the *5C's* has changed over many years. When I was growing up, my parents had more of a relationship with the people at their local bank. In those days, the people in the bank branch were well known to their clients and vice versa. Their kids went to the same schools and played on the same sports teams. The bankers had personal relationships with their clients outside of the branch. If they didn't know each other personally, they probably knew each others' older siblings or parents. The banking clients at that time were generational clients. Your grandparents banked there. Your parents banked there. So, you bank there. The *5C's* were used in a much different way at the time.

Capacity has always played a role, but the verification was much different. There was a really good chance the banker knew your supervisor or the owner of the company and would just make a quick verification call to confirm income and employment. The employer would gladly share because we didn't have the same privacy laws, either.

Character meant a lot more in the mortgage application back then. Who that person was carried a ton of value, and it was easy to verify because of the personal relationship. It wouldn't be uncommon for the branch manager to vouch for a mortgage applicant. It was normal to hear them say things like "Joe is a good man. I know his Dad and he won't let Joe miss his payments." The character component might even go as far back as the schoolyard where they'd grown up. The type of person people thought of us as was an important component.

The Collateral has always been an important component, but even that has changed considerably. Remember, the collateral is the actual home used as security for the mortgage. Recall that prior to the financial crash of 2009, home values in North America appeared to be skyrocketing and it seemed anyone could get approved for a mortgage. This is an example when too much emphasis was given to collateral. Institutions were lending money to people without income or jobs (capacity) simply because the speculation was the value of the home would appreciate so much that the lender would actually make money on a foreclosure by selling the home. These were referred to as NINJA loans, which stands for No Income No Job Applicants. There is a lot more to it than just this brief explanation, but it certainly demonstrates the point.

The value placed on the capital component has changed a little, as well. The future value of investments is completely speculative, and to base a lending decision on them would be irresponsible as a lender. Capital does tell part of the story, but not the whole story.

Credit has become the most important of the *5C's*. There are a ton of factors which contribute to why that is. Credit is an historical account of how we've handled our debt obligations in the past.

"We are what we repeatedly do. Excellence is not an act, but a habit."
- Will Durant

This quote from Will Durant pretty much explains why. When we look at the credit component of the *5C's*, it documents how you have handled your financial affairs in the past. The underwriters who review your mortgage application will use this as a predictor of how you may handle your affairs going forward. Now before you start jumping up and down ranting about what you did in the past does not determine what you will do in the future--that is only partly true. Have you ever tried to change a habit? It's hard. And we are not even aware of many habits. Changes can be made, but they take time and effort. You can certainly change your financial habits, but this also takes time and effort. That is one reason why there is so much emphasis on credit. The changes you make today will be reflected in your credit history over time.

"Credit scores have been very successful at predicting borrower risk and likelihood of default. Consider the 2008 Industry Home Equity Study, which looked at the percentage of people 90 or more days delinquent on their home equity loans. The results were as follows: 40.71% of those delinquent had a credit score below 619, 1.45% had a credit score of 620-739, and no one over a credit score of 740 were reported delinquent[xxii]. "

Past history is considered a good indicator of future performance. That probably does not come as a surprise to you. Have you ever run into a friend or acquaintance you haven't seen in five or six years and notice they are still doing the same things they were back then? Perhaps they jumped from job to job and are still doing that now. Maybe they're constantly struggling in relationships and the update you get five years later is that is still happening. It works the other way, too. A friend who was super ambitious and successful five years ago is still that way today.

Another reason credit has become the most important of the 5C's is changing technology. As access to computing power and information systems became more affordable and accessible, lenders began centralizing their underwriting departments. They also began implementing computer algorithms to score credit applications. The change we see today is we have no relationships with underwriters who review our applications as we did when the branch manager played on our softball team. The decision is going to be made by someone we will never meet and probably doesn't even live in the same city. They are using data to decide on the credit decision.

Technology is changing how these decisions are made. Artificial intelligence is changing the game rapidly. There are companies like First Access, a tech firm based in South Africa, who has developed software to underwrite credit applications based on mobile phone data and social profiles. Their algorithm pulls in data from mobile phone contacts and social profiles in addition to credit to assess the creditworthiness of an individual. Their positioning is data-driven credit.

The data won't care if you had a dispute with your mobile phone provider and the $230 phone bill you refused to pay was registered as a collection item on your credit report. The data won't care if you were only 10 days late on your last 10 credit card due dates and the data won't care if you are carrying all your credit cards at maximum because you are waiting for your annual bonus. They all have an impact on your credit.

If you look forward over the next five-to-six years, the credit component is only going to become more critical as lenders implement technology to use data to assess your capacity and character in addition to credit. They will be able to link ALL of our attributes to how we pay. That also means that as a first-time homebuyer or even a repeat buyer, you'll need to take care of your credit today.

The role of credit will determine

- o Your ability to acquire credit to buy your home; whether it's your first home or your next home
- o The price you will pay and the terms that can be offered

If you have good credit, do everything you can to keep it that way. If you have some credit blemishes, do everything you can to make amends and continue your path to re-establishing yourself. If you have poor credit, all is not lost. It is simply a matter of managing your reality gap. Just like changing a habit, repairing your credit takes time and work.

The Default Insurance Misnomer

If the 5C's of credit is the most misunderstood subject among first-time or repeat home buyers, default insurance is the second. This topic is so poorly explained to mortgage customers that I felt it is worth revisiting it as one of the most important topics to know.

To recap, Canadian lenders can only provide mortgage financing to qualified homeowners with at least a 20% down payment, unless the mortgage is insured against default by law.

Over the years, I have helped thousands of clients with their mortgages and I meet very few who understand the terms of the default insurance requirements. I understand there are first-time homebuyers who have little to no knowledge on the subject, but I also meet a disproportionate share of repeat home buyers who don't know much about default insurance.

Let me clear the air about some misunderstandings about default insurance.

A. The requirement for default insurance is not determined on if you are a first-time homebuyer.

It does not matter if you are a first-time homebuyer or have bought many homes. The requirement for default insurance is based on the size of the down payment and not the history of the borrower. Default insurance is required on any residential mortgage with less than a 20% down payment. There are no exceptions to this rule. If a borrower is only able to provide 19% as a down payment, the mortgage will require default insurance.

For example, a home buyer is buying a home for a $500,000 purchase price and has a $50,000 down payment (10%) will require default insurance. If the same home buyer is buying that home for $500,000 and has a $100,000 down payment (20%), they will not be required to have default insurance.

Another way to phrase this is using Loan-to-Value (LTV). The Loan-to-Value is the ratio of how much of the market value is mortgaged. A 20% down payment is the same effect as an 80% Loan-to-Value. A mortgage which has 80% LTV or LESS, does not require default insurance.

B. Your application must be approved by the lender AND the insurer.

When a mortgage has less than a 20% down payment and requires default insurance, the mortgage application will need to be approved by the lender AND the insurer. There are three insurers in Canada: Canadian Mortgage Housing Corporation (CMHC), Genworth Canada and Canada Guaranty. The insurer will evaluate every application using their underwriting guidelines to approve or decline the default insurance. Underwriting requirements at the insurer are very closely aligned to that of the lenders, so very few applications are approved by one and declined by the other. However, lenders are free to approve any mortgage application (based on their underwriting requirements) they choose, provided the borrower has at least a 20% down payment or the LTV is 80% or less.

C. Default insurance protects the lender, not the borrower.

There are very few insurances a consumer can buy and pay for which don't protect their interests. Default insurance is one of them. The premium for default insurance when it is required because the minimum down payment is insufficient is paid for the borrower. The premium can either be paid out of pocket or be added to the mortgage.

When a bank forecloses on a mortgage which is insured, the insurer pays the lender the balance of the debt, but this does not absolve the borrower of the obligation. The foreclosure will be registered on the borrower's credit report and the insurer will continue to pursue other remedies depending on the situation.

D. Default insurance may still be required even the borrower has a 20% (or more) as downpayment.

Lenders may require the borrower to buy default insurance even if the minimum 20% down payment is provided. The default insurance reduces the risk to the lender and can be used to offset it. One situation where this may be required are homes in remote locations. It is not common for lenders to require default insurance when it is not required, but it can happen.

A mortgage which is insured versus uninsured can have an impact beyond the cost of the premium.

Down Payment		
20% or more	Uninsurable (Conventional)	• Access to longer amortization periods • No insurer premium • Higher mortgage interest rates
Less than 20%	Insurable (High Ratio)	• Maximum 25 year amortization • Borrower pays insurer premium • Lower mortgage interest rates

Having or not having a 20% down payment can affect more than just the requirement for default insurance. A conventional mortgage can get access to longer amortization periods and do not pay the insurer premium as already mentioned. The challenge is that since the lender is required to take on the risk of the mortgage, they will charge a higher interest rate on the mortgage.

On the other side of that coin, a high-ratio mortgage can benefit from a lower interest rate because the lender is passing the mortgage risk on to the insurer. The drawbacks are that insurers will limit the amortization to a maximum of 25 years and the borrower has to pay the premium.

It's no wonder homebuyers, first-time or repeat, are so confused and would rather not deal with it. It really is a between-a-rock-and-a-hard-place kind of situation, especially if you want a longer amortization to get a lower payment.

There are alternative strategies. For example, a home buyer who has a 20% down payment may choose to insure the mortgage to get the benefit of a lower interest rate as long as the lower rate offsets the cost of the premium. A home buyer who only has $50,000 as a down payment may opt to buy a home for $250,000 instead of $500,000, which increases the ratio of their down payment to 20% instead of 10%, giving them the benefit of a longer amortization and avoiding the insurer premium.

This isn't everything you need to know about default insurance. It's just enough to give you an understanding so you can ask better questions and put yourself in a better position to make a good decision.

The Big Take Away

My point is this. There is a ton of information out there about mortgages and buying your Big Asset that you need to know and can learn. This seems like a lot, and it is. It doesn't matter if you are a first-time homebuyer or have gone through this process before. The information and data changes, which is why I want you to have a good general understanding. From time-to-time, the rules of the game may change. If you understand the underlying principles, you will ALWAYS be able to figure out the game.

There was a lot to absorb about how the *5C's* of credit and default insurance have changed and how each will affect you as you venture into to buying your first home or your next home. There is still lots to learn about ALL the different mortgage products available to you so you can work with your professional mortgage advisor and put together an effective plan. I introduced you to rates and terms back in Chapter Seven. Here, I would like to take you into a deeper dive on what these mean for you and how they may affect your homebuying plan.

Products and Terms

Just to clarify, when lenders, mortgage brokers or other industry professionals refer to products or terms with respect to mortgaging your home, this is what they mean:

Products - The mortgage used to finance your home. The product is provided by the lender and usually refers to the interest rate and type. For example, the rate type is either fixed or variable and the rate is expressed as an annual percentage rate or A.P.R.

Terms - The terms really mean the mortgage term, amortization period and type. The mortgage term can be anywhere from six months to 10 years. This is the period for which the products will be contracted. The amortization period is the schedule for payments and can range up to 30 years. And finally, the term type is either open or closed.

If you are a first-time homebuyer, all of this may feel overwhelming. That is exactly why I wrote this book. There is a lot of information to digest. Look at it this way--it's not necessary for you to know every little in and out of the products and terms. That's why you have a professional mortgage advisor. You just need enough background information to be able to instruct your advisor how to work with you. You will be much better at communicating your needs with your advisor and their team, which in turn means they will be able to offer only the solutions which make sense for you.

You may be a repeat buyer and might even have a general understanding of some of what I have been writing about, although in my experience, many repeat buyers can use a lot more knowledge. Either way, I am quite certain if your last home purchase was prior to Jan 2018, things have changed. The government regulations have changed and so have the programs.

Whichever category you find yourself in today, please pay particular attention to this section. Until now, I have only presented general concepts and a little detail about how some of these programs work. Please do not feel like you have to memorize all of the details here or think you need a thesis-level knowledge on these topics. My goal for you here is to prepare you for your next conversation with your mortgage advisor. If you are able to say, "Yes, I remember reading about that," and understand your advisor's recommendations, I will consider that a win.

Products

The product is actually quite easy to understand when you break it down into its parts. Remember, I like things to be simple. The product is just the rate type and the corresponding A.P.R. There are only two rate types--Fixed and Variable. Easy, right? The part that overwhelms most people are the number of corresponding rates for fixed and variable. There are tons! One major mortgage lender in Canada has approximately 13 different rates posted on their website as of the writing of this book. Multiply that by 20-30 different mortgage lenders and it's no wonder consumers feel frustrated.

Let's make this simple. I mentioned previously that the best mortgage isn't necessarily the one with the best rate. It's the one which provides you the most value. Rate is just a small part of it. And there are strategies to mitigate the rate.

So back to simple and the two rate types.

Variable Rate

The first thing to understand about variable rates is how they are calculated. The variable rates posted by the lenders are usually expressed as their base rate plus (+ or minus (- an adjustment. For example, you may read a variable rate as Lender Prime + 1.5% or Lender Prime - 0.25%. What makes these rates variable is that the Lender Prime, also referred to as the base rate, will be adjusted from time to time. The lender will increase or decrease their base rate depending on what their economists have to say about a lot of different factors including:

- GDP
- Employment Rates
- Credit Defaults
- Profitability
- Inflation
- Bank of Canada Prime

These factors, along with others, determine where the lender will set their base rate. The primary driver is the Bank of Canada Prime rate. This is the rate that the chartered banks will pay to borrow their money from the government. There are five chartered banks in Canada. All other lenders will still adjust their base rate along with the prime rate even though they have a different source of capital. The amount of the adjustment they make depends on who is backing them. For either group, the way they make money is through spread. The difference between the rate the Bank of Canada (or other source charges them and the rate they charge you.

The rate spread has dropped considerably since the 1930's, where the average decade spreads have been[xxiii]

1930s	1940s	1950s	1960s	1970s	1980s	1990s	2000s
2.62%	2.87%	2.16%	1.23%	1.16%	1.21%	1.24%	1.55%

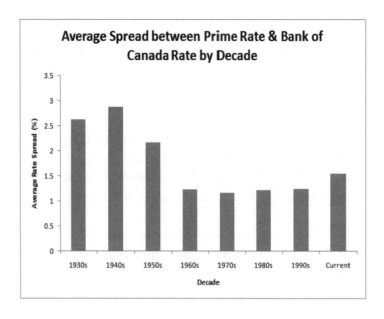

The reason I share this with you is to help create an understanding about why banking works the way it does. This is all about my favourite radio station - the WIIFM. Have you heard of it before?

WIIFM = What's in It for Me?

When we understand not merely how the lenders are motivated (profit) but how they earn their profits, we can put ourselves in a much better position. As you read in the last chapter, and can probably guess from this chapter, the variable rate fluctuates. As a borrower, it is important for your own financial and personal well-being that you understand that fact and know what your own comfort level is, regardless if you are first-time homebuyer or repeat buyer. The posted variable rates are typically lower than the fixed rates. So if you simply go shopping for a mortgage based on finding the lowest rate, you could find yourself in the very uncomfortable position of trying to deal with a higher mortgage payment because of a rate hike. If you didn't factor the fluctuation into your plan, this could result in a tremendous amount of stress on your bank account and your family.

Now you have a high-level understanding of what a variable rate is and how it is calculated.

Fixed Rates

The fixed rate uses another financial instrument as a pricing index similar to the variable rate. Though fixed rates use the government bonds as a benchmark instead of the Bank of Canada prime rate. There isn't much more detail needed about how fixed rate is determined.

When you choose a fixed rate for your mortgage, your payment will not change for the entire term of your mortgage agreement. This could be between 1-10 years. Your rate and payment stay fixed. I like it when things are simple. A majority of mortgages today are fixed. If this is in your comfort zone, you're not alone.
Just be aware that there are trade offs for certainty as I wrote in chapter 7. You will pay more for a fixed rate mortgage. Historically, posted variable rates have been lower than 5-year fixed rates (undiscounted[xxiv]).

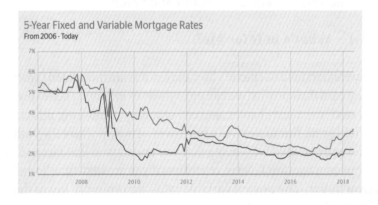

5-Year Fixed and Variable Mortgage Rates
From 2006 - Today

As you can tell from the chart above, the variable rates have almost always been lower than fixed except for a brief period in 2007. Before that, you would have to go back to the mid 80's to find a time when the posted variable rate was more than the fixed. The interest difference is what you will pay for the payment certainty.

Best of Both Worlds????

What if you could get the benefits of an interest rate discount using variable but get the payment certainty of a fixed rate?

This is not a trick question and is very possible!

The strategy to apply here would be to set up a payment which is more than your minimum payment under the variable rate. When a rate increase occurs, your payment will absorb the increase. Your payment stays constant. This does come with a warning--it does not protect you from change in payments in all scenarios. This will depend on the payment you set up on your variable-rate mortgage.

For example, suppose your variable rate payment is $1200/month and you want a fixed payment of $1500 per month. Month after month, you are paying your $1500/m as scheduled and you get a 30-day notification that a rate change is coming. This rate change will cause your variable rate payment ($1200/m) to increase by $150. However, you set up a fixed payment of $1500 so that doesn't change. The part which changes is how much of your payment is contributed to principal. After the rate increase, $150 more of your $1500 payment will go toward interest.

As long as the combination of rate increases (and decreases) never results in a change in payment to be more than $1500, your payment will never change. However, the risk is that a rate change or series of increases can move your payment to be more than the fixed payment you set up. In that scenario, you will be required to pay the new payment. For example, if over the last 12 months you have received three notices of rate increases. The total of which is an overall increase of $450 per month. Your payment will increase to $1650 per month.

Using the plan from Chapter Five will help you to decide what the right amount is to set up as a fixed payment and how much of a rate increase you could absorb. This sounds far less frustrating and worrisome than just rolling the dice, doesn't it?

Terms

The second piece of your mortgage agreement are the terms. The terms include:

o Mortgage Term
o Amortization Period
o Term Type

Mortgage Term

The mortgage term is the length of time the rate and the term type will cover. The term is between six months to 10 years. The rate is usually quoted along with the term, such as a five-year fixed or a five-year variable. Thinking about how the lenders know which rate they will offer with which term is a function of WIIFM. Their decision is ultimately based on profit and risk.

Back to the term. Before you decide on which term is right for you, you need to make a decision about your exit strategy. This sounds strange, doesn't it? Why would I need to consider how I am going to get out of this mortgage when I haven't even started the mortgage? Here are a couple of examples to explain:

Jim and Susan are a young couple who have just finished traveling in Asia for a year after they finished their University degrees. They've both just started their careers and are planning to get married within the next year and start a family. They want to buy their first home and need some help figuring out the best solution for them. They can afford to get into a nice starter home in a good neighborhood. They would even consider a condo for the two of them. They want to have one baby soon after they are married and then two more children within the next couple of years.

Choosing the wrong term may cost them a lot of money and headaches. If they choose too short a term, they may be overpaying in interest and renewal fees. If they choose too long a term, they will either be stuck in a home which no longer suits them or they'll have to pay high payout penalties. What should they do? A three-year term would work well for them. If they take a year to live in their starter home (or even condo) while the work and get married, and then a year in which to have their first child, it will be at least another year before they have their second and third children and outgrow their first home.

Sam is a wealthy executive and has worked hard his entire career. He and his wife have successfully raised four children, all of whom are out of the house. He and his wife travel for four months of the year and they have no need for such a large house for themselves, especially when they are gone so often. Sam and his wife are downgrading their home for something smaller in another part of the city. He will have a sizable down payment and doesn't want to have to worry about a large mortgage payment. He would like to take advantage of some cheaper rates. They will sell again when he retires in about 10 years and buy his dream home.

Sam has a long-term exit on this new property he will be buying so a short term is not necessary. Though it's not going to be his retirement home, they will be there for a while. The term which would suit Sam and his wife would be five years. This term will give Sam his best rate options AND fit with his exit plans.

The right terms are somewhat subjective and very strategic. The message is you are trying to predict an unpredictable future. As much as the mortgage industry changes, your life changes, too. The goal here is to build in as much flexibility as possible based on what you think you might do. Finding the right term is a key to saving you time, money, and frustration.

Brett Roessel

Amortization Period

The amortization period is the length of time over which your mortgage will be paid. The average amortization is between 25-30 years. The maximum amortization is 30 years and can be as low as 10 years. Once your purchase price and down payment have been planned, the amortization combined with the rate will determine the amount of the payment. The longer the amortization period, the lower the payment.

Here's the rub. The longer the amortization period, the more interest you will pay. The additional interest may be substantial because of compounding. The other side of the coin is interest may significantly be reduced with a shorter amortization period[xxv].

Short vs. Long Amortization Periods

	Scenario A (25 Years)	Scenario B (30 years)	The Difference
Mortgage amount	$300,000	$300,000	
Amortization period	25 Years	30 Years	5 Years
Interest rate	3.49%	3.49%	
Monthly payment	$1,496	$1,341	$155
Total interest paid over entire loan	$148,868	$182,854	$33,986

Take a look at the comparison above. The difference between a 25-year and a 30-year mortgage is only $155 per month but will cost an extra $33,986 in interest for the longer term. Let's do the math. The $155 per month over the five-year difference is only $9300, but the total extra costs (or savings if you go the other way) is over $33K. When choosing your amortization, how much are you willing to spend and is it worth it?

> **Learning Lesson**
> Any mortgage with a down payment less than 20% must carry default insurance. The maximum amortization is 25 years for high ratio mortgages. Down payment and default insurance affect your options for the amortization period and subsequently, your payment.

Term Type

The final decision you will need to make as a homebuyer is the term type. Again, I like things to be simple. There are only two options for term types: open or closed. The two differences between open and closed are the prepayment privileges and the interest rate. In short, an open term has no payout penalty (except for any administration fees to cover the cost of discharge), while a closed term does. An open-term mortgage has a higher interest rate than a closed.

The open term is quite simple and only needs a little explanation. All the prepayment privileges I listed in Chapter Five apply to open-term mortgages, PLUS the balance can be paid out at any time without penalty.

> **Learning Lesson**
> Why do open terms have a higher interest rate then closed terms?
>
> Think about the WIIFM from a lenders perspective. They make their money from collecting interest on the money they lend to you. An open term mortgage can be paid out at any time without penalty. That means you will save the interest by paying out the mortgage. Which also means the lender will not make the interest they counted on. The lender charges a higher rate on open term mortgages to compensate for the potential lost interest if you pay out the mortgage early.

The closed term requires a little more explanation. The closed-term limits the prepayment privileges of the borrower. When you choose a closed-term mortgage, you are agreeing to carry the mortgage the full length of the term. Lenders will offer a lower interest rate for these types of mortgages. The consequence of paying out the mortgage before the end of the term is the payout penalty. There are some exemptions called prepayment privileges (see Chapter Five) but are dependent on the lender. Some lenders will restrict these privileges or not offer them at all.

The payout penalty is an interest calculation based on your rate and principal balance. The penalties are calculated as the greater of either

- 3-months of interest
- Interest Differential (IRD)

Three-Months' Interest

The first of the two interest penalty calculations is relatively simple. The three-months' interest calculation is the principal balance times the APR divided by 4 (the number of 3-month quarters in the year).

Principal Mortgage Balance	X	Annual Percentage Rate*	÷	4	=	3-Month Interest Penalty

For example, Jim and Sue have a large lump sum of money they earned from the proceeds in the sale of their business and would like to pay out their mortgage. Their current principal balance is $170,000 and their contract rate is 3.64%. The 3-months interest calculation is as follows:

$170,000 x 3.64% = $6188 annual interest / 4 = **$1547**

This calculation is still only an approximation. The most accurate calculation will come directly from your lender. Remember the WIIFM?

The lenders will want to recover as much of the interest as possible and will calculate the interest to the day. Their interest quote will even add in a time buffer of 10-15 days to account for the time it takes to process the principal repayment.

*** WARNING ***

You must make sure you are informed about this calculation! While most lenders will use your contract rate to calculate the three-months' interest, some may have contracted to use the posted rate if it's higher. What if Jim and Sue's mortgage agreement outlined that the three-month's interest calculation uses the higher rate between the contracted and the posted rate? It is possible the interest calculation could be higher.

For example, Jim & Sue's mortgage agreement was written so they will need to use the posted rate to calculate the three-months' interest calculation, which happens to be +1.77% higher.

$170,000 x (3.64%+1.77%) = $9197 annual interest / 4 = **$2299.25**

The difference is over $752! Just another reason why it is so important for you to be informed AND work with a competent mortgage professional.

Interest Rate Differential (IRD)

While the three-months' interest calculation is relatively simple, the interest rate differential may feel like a bit of a black hole calculation for many people. This isn't really surprising. The calculation keeps changing. First of all, the IRD calculation can vary between lenders. Secondly, the comparison rates are always changing.

Here are a few factors which can affect the amount of interest penalty you may have to pay when IRD is used:

○ Do you have any pre-payment privileges available which can be used to reduce the principal mortgage amount used in the calculation without penalty?

- Does your lender round up your remaining months to the next closest term when determining your comparison rate?
- Does your lender round down your remaining months?
- Which posted rate will your lender use for comparison?

I can understand why for many people this feels so disruptive. It's a moving target and no one is telling you where to aim--until now. As I have mentioned directly and alluded to throughout this book, my only goal here is to give you information to increase your understanding. When you have an understanding of the background about why these instruments work the way they do, the better the questions you can ask.

One example of a standard IRD calculation is your existing mortgage rate minus your lender's current rate closest to your remaining term multiplied by your mortgage balance times your remaining term. Simple right???? Don't stress out if you just read that sentence and all you saw was *blah blah blah.*

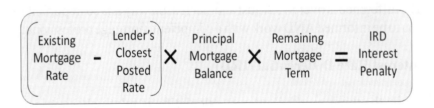

Let's use the same example from Jim and Sue in the 3-month interest calculation:

- $170,000 principal
- 3.64% contract rate
- 5.41% lender's closest posted rate
- 2-year remaining term (new information)

(3.64% - 5.41%) x $170,000 = $3009 annual interest x 2 years = **$6018**

*** **IMPORTANT NOTE**: This calculation is ONLY an estimate of the interest calculation. The only certain method to get an accurate quote on the interest rate differential is to get it from your lender. Just don't take their word for it. Compare their calculation to the one outlined in your mortgage agreement working with your mortgage professional. There can be multiple methods for this calculation which all depend on your lender's conditions and the timing of your early payout.

How does that calculation compare to the three-months' interest calculation? It's not just a little more. It's A LOT more! This just reinforces my message about understanding what you're getting into. There is too much at stake here for you and your family. Remember, it's not necessarily how much money you make, but it's about how much money you get to keep.

It Ain't About the Rate!

Let's take this a little deeper for understanding. From the previous discussion, you now know variable rates are generally lower than fixed rates and closed terms are generally lower than open terms. If all you did was shop different lenders for the lowest possible rate, you would most likely end up with a five-year closed variable rate (or some variation depending on the lender). Everything comes with a price. The lowest possible rate you are seeking comes with trade-offs.

Here is a recap of many factors you need to consider in your overall plan *in addition to* the size of the interest rate:

What is the most likely length of time you are planning to be in your home?
How high or low is your tolerance for fluctuations in your monthly payment?
How much is the down payment you can provide?
What is the mortgage amount you can comfortably afford based on your income today?
What is the current status of your credit history?
How much is your personal net worth and what is the liquidity of your current financial assets?
Are you planning any major life events that may affect your mortgage situation? (e.g. children, wedding, etc.)
Do you have a need or desire to pay down any additional principal during your term?

All of these questions and many others should be answered as part of your mortgage plan to determine the right product and terms to fit YOU! The lenders are going to offer the services which work best for them and are competitive, though depending on your circumstances, not ALL products and terms will be competitive. There are hundreds of combinations of lenders, products and terms. Your ability to provide your professional mortgage advisor with as much relevant details as possible is the only way to ensure you find the best deal that works for YOU!

A misstep in choosing the right product and term to fit your financial goals and objectives can cost you many thousands of dollars sometime down the road. I am not trying to scare you or make the process of financing your Big Asset intimidating. This discussion may come across that way. My real goal here is to make sure you are informed. Buying a home, regardless if it's your first or your fifth, should be an exciting an enjoyable experience. I feel when homebuyers are adequately informed, they can be more open to enjoy the journey instead of having stress or worry about everything they don't know about the biggest purchase most will make in their lifetime.

A Second Look at The Home Buyers Plan (HBP)

We discussed the Home Buyers Plan back in Chapter Four and is worthy of a reprisal. Recall that the HBP is a federal government program which enables homebuyers who qualify to withdraw up to $25,000 from their RRSP tax free, provided the money is paid back into the RRSP over the following 15 years.

Here is why you should care. According to Trading Economics[xxvi], the national household savings rate is 4.4% of gross income while the median household income from 2016 census data was $70,336[xxvii]. Putting this all together, this means Canadian households are only saving approximately $258 per month. This lines up somewhat with CIBC's poll in 2017[xxviii] which revealed "82% admit they could 'cut back' each month by on average $360 before feeling the pinch."

A 5% deposit on a $500,000 home would require $25,000 in savings. If you decided to 'save-your-way' to your down payment, it would take you over eight years to save a $25K down payment if you were similar to the average Canadian, who is only saving 4.4% of his gross income, or $258 monthly. That's great news if you are planning to buy a home in just over eight years!

I know you save better than the average Canadian and you are able to 'cut back' an extra $360 per month before you feel the pinch. It will take just over three years to save the $25K down payment. This sounds like a much better deal!

Or you can take advantage of the Home Buyers Plan if you already have the $25K in your RRSP and have your down payment ready in a couple of days.

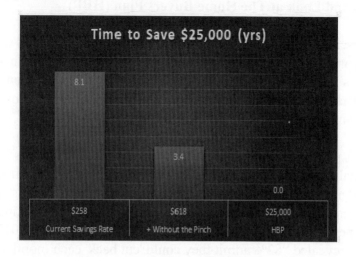

Here is another way to look at using your RRSP in the Home Buyers Plan. Borrow your down payment from your RRSP today and re-contribute...

- o $618 per month to repay in 3.4 years
- o $258 per month to repay in 8.1 years
- o $139 per month to repay in 15 years*

*   Under the HBP, the Government of Canada only requires your RRSP to be paid back at a rate of 1/15 every year over 15 years.

> **RRSP Meltdown Strategy**
> The HBP may also be a suitable RRSP meltdown strategy that some qualified candidates can use to liquidate their RRSP's.
>
> Instead of re-paying the minimum 1/15th back to their RRSP under the HBP, it may be suitable to claim that amount on that year's income tax return as income. Depending on the individual's total income for the year, the taxes owed on the additional income may be less than if re-paid and claimed in future years.
>
> DISCLAIMER: Author is not a financial adviser. You should consider seeking independent legal, financial, taxation or other advice to check how the information relates to your unique circumstances. Author is not liable for any loss caused, whether due to negligence or otherwise arising from the use of, or reliance on, the information provided directly or indirectly, of this statement.

Do you think that the HBP can assist you to get into your home sooner rather than three-to-eight years down the road? Absolutely.

What's the Catch?

The first catch is you must have the RRSP savings. The HBP program does not include funds in any other types of saving vehicles, such as non-registered/open investments or permanent tax shelters. You must have funds withdrawn from your RRSP.

Second, there are qualifications[xxix]. You must meet three eligibility requirements:

1. Must be considered a first-time homebuyer.
2. Have a written agreement to buy or build a qualifying home for yourself.
3. You must intend to occupy in the qualifying home as your principal place of residence within one year after buying or building it.

Are You an Eligible First-Time Homebuyer?

Eligibility as a 'first-time' homebuyer is a bit misleading. You can qualify for the HBP even if this is your second, third or Nth home. You can qualify for the HBP if you did not occupy a home you or your current spouse owned in the past four-year period.

The four-year period begins on January 1 of the 4th year before you withdraw the funds and ends 31 days before the date you withdraw the funds. For example, if you sold your home in 2014, you would be eligible to participate in the HBP in 2019. You can find more information about the HBP on the Canadian Revenue Agency's website at: https://www.canada.ca/home.html

This program and its rules demonstrate how important it is that you have a plan! You could be leaving valuable options and flexibility behind simply because you didn't have the information available to you. It also shows the importance of having a competent and trustworthy mortgage professional with whom to work. The earlier in the process you can involve your mortgage professional, the better deal you will have and the less stress you will experience. You need to have a team with whom to work as you buy your home--You, your Real Estate Agent, and your Mortgage Professional.

Buying Today is Not the Same as it was Yesterday

If you bought a home within the last eight months (at least at the time of the writing of this book), mortgaging the purchase of your home has already changed. It is even likely to change by the time you buy your next home. That's why I say buying your home today is not the same as it was yesterday. Even if you are buying your first home and going through the experience for the first time, you may have a network of people who have and are ready to give you a ton of advice. I am also certain the rules have changed since they last mortgaged their homes.

That should be pretty apparent from what you read in Chapter Four. The industry regularly changes its products and terms and the government regularly changes its regulations.
It doesn't matter if you bought your home in the last eight months or eight years. The requirements have changed. Not just a little. They have changed a lot.

Just 10 years ago, a homebuyer could shop for a 40-year mortgage. Imagine in what position today's homebuyer finds themselves if they signed a 40-year mortgage 10 years ago and wanted to buy again today? They would have 30 years left on their current mortgage. Depending on their credit and the size of their down payment, they may only qualify for a max 25-year mortgage, which doesn't provide that home buyer with very many options.

Just 10 years ago, a home refinance could be written for up to 95% of the current market value of the home. Today, that figure has dropped to a maximum of 80%. A homebuyer used to be able to finance a home purchase using a home equity line of credit at 80% of the market value. Today it is a maximum of 65%.

The lenders have also changed their decision criteria. Confirming a borrower's income used to only require a recent pay stub and possibly a letter from the employer. Today, verifying income likely requires a pay stub, an employer letter and notice of assessment going back two years.

Things change. Whether for better or for worse, they change. It is in your best interest to make sure you are informed. As I mentioned before, it is worth many thousands of dollars to you. The good news is, you don't have to be the one to read all of the legislation, industry literature and all the other requirements from the 40+ lenders. That's the power of having a professional mortgage advisor on your team.

Ideas to Remember

○   The two different rate types are variable or fixed.

○   The payment can change with a variable-rate product while stays the same with a fixed-rate product.

○   A fixed payment can be structured using a variable rate.

○   A mortgage term is either open or closed.

○   Early payout on a closed-term mortgage will require an interest penalty of either three-months' or Interest Rate Differential (IRD), whichever is greater.

○   Choose a mortgage product and term which fits with your plan. Shopping on rates alone can leave you exposed.

○   First-time homebuyers and repeat buyers can take advantage of the Home Buyers Plan if they meet eligibility requirements.

○   Mortgage products, terms, regulations, and conditions are constantly changing.

CHAPTER NINE
WHAT NOW

*"Often when you think you're at the end of something,
you're at the beginning of something else."*

~ Fred Rogers

You've met with your chosen mortgage professional and set up your plan. You've shared your plan with your real estate professional and have gone on the hunt for your perfect home. After a few short weeks, you've found it! Your almost-perfect home. *This is a great house* you think to yourself. It's in the area we wanted with a fantastic yard AND a garage. BONUS! It's not quite the kitchen you wanted but your mortgage professional showed you how you can finance the remodeling into your mortgage and ensured you were pre-approved for it. So you have no worries.

You made a fair offer to the seller and they accepted! It's so exciting. Your professional team takes you through the entire process to complete the necessary paperwork. There were a few items which needed follow-up, but you had built a great plan with your mortgage professional, so the issues were quickly resolved.

Moving Day!
You had a successful walkthrough and it's time to move in after a short possession meeting. A few close friends came to help you move in and see your new house. It was also a nice time to catch up and have a few drinks and pizza on the backyard deck of your new home after the job is done.

A few weeks have gone by and you are totally moved in, unpacked, and settled in your new home. Congratulations!

This is the beginning and not the end of your journey with your Big Asset.

"When you're done saving for my education, don't forget to start saving for my retirement."

The closing date is not the last time you should see your mortgage professional. There is still work to do. You have lifelong plans and circumstances will change. Sometimes they will grow and get better. You will get a promotion, make more money, or grow your family. Sometimes you may be challenged. You might be faced with a family emergency, job loss or other distress. Whatever circumstances comes your way, your mortgage professional is there to celebrate with you or help you to get out of a jam.

Your mortgage professional does more than help you design your plan and then get you into your home. They are there to help you FULLY execute your plan to the end. Since your plan never really ends, the same is said about the service from your mortgage professional. You should expect, nay, demand an after-closing follow-up schedule. You wouldn't put $200,000 or more into a stock or other investment and not have the advisor check-in with you once in awhile to update you on how it's going. You shouldn't settle for that when investing this amount of money into the single biggest purchase you will probably ever make in your lifetime, either.

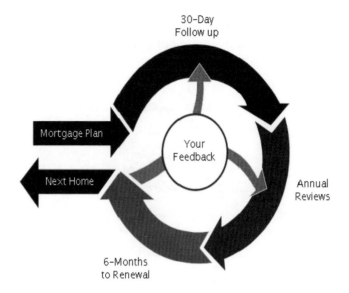

The mortgage plan and execution are the processes you just went through to open this chapter and the end of that process is the beginning of the next. Sometime within the next **30-45 days**, you will want to sit down with your professional mortgage advisor for a quick review. Over the next three-to-five years, or however long a term you set up in your plan, you should be meeting with your advisor at least once per year for an **Annual Review**. Towards the end of your term, you and your advisor should sit down six months prior to your **Renewal**. Each step serves a specific purpose to make sure you stay on track with your plan and achieve all your financial objectives.

30-Day Follow-Up

The 30-day (up to 45-day) follow-up is a very important time. Up to this point, you have received a TON of information and had to make a lot of decisions. It probably felt a lot like drinking from a fire hose-maybe even drinking from several at the same time! Most likely, you may have forgotten some the details of your mortgage, even though you understood the terms at the time. That's quite normal.

There are a lot that demands your attention while you are designing and executing your plan with your professional mortgage advisor, shopping for a home with your real estate agent and then within the excitement of closing the deal. It's natural to forget most of the information you were given. That doesn't mean it is a good idea to lock your papers away in a filing cabinet somewhere not to be touched for the next 25-30 years. Quite the opposite is true.

Amortization Schedule

Within the first 30-45 days, your executed mortgage agreement and amortization schedule will be delivered to your lawyer, who will then pass it on to you. That is your signal to book an appointment with your professional mortgage advisor to review the schedule and documents.

The amortization schedule will detail the payment terms of your agreement. It will outline the...

- Periodic payment (weekly, biweekly, monthly, etc.)
- Breakdown of principal and interest for each payment
- Schedule of payments over the amortization period
- Payment due dates
- Contracted interest rate
- Total interest to be paid

General Terms and Conditions

I know what you're thinking. Who wants to sit and read a 60-70-page finance agreement cover to cover? Isn't that why we have lawyers and professional mortgage advisors involved? Well, yes and no. There really is no substitute for you to read every agreement you sign and question the terms you don't understand. The 30-Day Follow-Up will be a great opportunity to review the documents with your advisor and clarify any terms you may have forgotten since the closing.

Your advisor will discuss the product (fixed or variable) and the term (closed or open) along with any other items important for you to know. For example, if you are signed to a variable rate, you should understand your payment can change and how that may affect your amortization schedule. If your agreement is a closed term, you will want to review all your prepayment privileges along with any payout penalties written into the agreement.

Who to Call?

The 30-Day Follow-Up is the best time to review who you should call if you need any changes. The lender's information will be detailed in the paperwork, though some organizations can be very large and have many offices or departments, depending on who you need to reach. You may need to update your banking information to change which account you use to make your mortgage payments. Perhaps you need to change payment dates or update phone numbers.

You can always contact your advisor for help, but it is helpful to know where to go when they are unavailable.

Any Other Stuff

This is a fantastic time to ask all those questions you didn't ask before your closing but wished you had. Believe it or not, many people are afraid to ask important questions because they are made to feel they should already know the answers. This often happens when a group of professionals such as real estate agents, lawyers, lenders, and mortgage advisors talk about a home purchase as if it is an everyday occurrence. To them, it is. They deal with many transactions every day and sometimes forget you do not have the same level of exposure. Even if you have purchased a home in the past and have the experience of the process, they may make you feel as if you should already know what is going on. As much as we try to flush out any questions you have and make clear your understanding, some items are bound to fall through the cracks. The 30-Day Follow-Up is the second-best time to ask those questions and get clarification.

The 30-Day Follow-Up is a chance to revisit your plan after the excitement of purchasing your Big Asset has worn off a little bit and you can think with a clear mind. Not to mention, it's also nice to be able to celebrate the occasion with your advisor in your new home.

Annual Review

Huzzahhhh! It's been about one year since you bought your home. You have done some serious living over the last 12-14 months and everything feels normal. The newness of where you live has worn off. You have developed all new routines, such as the time you get up and get ready for work to the routes you take to get there. The local grocery store has become your new go-to and you probably even have a couple of new favorite restaurants close to where you now live. Life continues to happen--as normal as it can be for anyone.

The first annual review is one of the most important meetings after you have purchased your Big Asset. For many, it feels unnecessary or redundant. After all, you have been making payments on your mortgage, your budget for household expenses is relatively consistent and life is pretty good. What is there to discuss? The short answer is--a lot.

At some point shortly after your one-year anniversary, you will receive a mortgage statement which details all your payments, along with the amount of principal and interest you've paid. I need to warn you about a couple of things that will happen:

○ **Prepare to get a little bit of sticker shock.**

> The amount of interest paid compared to the amount of principal will look very slanted in favor of the lender. The reason it looks that way is because the interest is front-end loaded in the mortgage payment schedule. Part of the reason is to offset the risk the lender takes. The biggest risk to the lender is in the first 1/3 of the mortgage so the repayment and interest reflects that.

> The other reason is not as well-known or openly discussed because it maximizes the profit for the lender. Remember our entire discussion of WIIFM? The lenders are in the business of making a profit by financing mortgages, which is to be expected. In fact, we want them to be able to make profit. As a society, profitable companies benefit our economy so they can continue to pay employees who want to buy things. If the mortgage business wasn't profitable, where would you find a lender to purchase your home?

o **You may be a little over whelmed.**

There are a ton of details in your mortgage statement, all of which are important, though not every detail will have an immediate impact on you today. Each lender has their own format for issuing your mortgage statement, but each of them will include details about your rate, your payment, the principal balance, the mortgage term, and amortization. Some of this information should be familiar if you and your professional mortgage advisor have had a good plan since the beginning. If you didn't spend much time on your plan or didn't have a plan at all, your statement will look a lot more confusing than it needs to be.

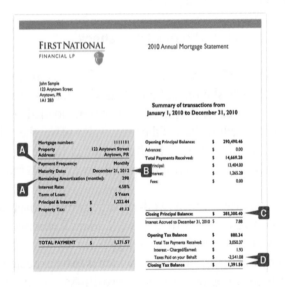

The primary purpose of your annual review is to compare the past year's results with your original plan. If you and your professional mortgage advisor set you up on a fixed-rate closed mortgage without any prepayment privileges, your statement should appear as expected.

If your mortgage was written with ANY variable conditions, such as interest rate or prepayments, you will want to pay particular attention to the details.

Changes in the Base Rate

From time to time, the base mortgage rate may change throughout the year. The Bank of Canada can choose to raise/lower their base rate, the lenders can choose to raise/lower their base rate or any combination of either can happen. Regardless if you are in a fixed or variable-rate product, you will want to know how this can affect you.

For a fixed-rate mortgage, the impact for you will be subtle. Any changes in the base rate will not impact your mortgage at the time. That doesn't mean you should ignore it. At some point, you are going to renew your mortgage, and a series of consecutive and substantial base-rate increases may leave you with an unexpectedly high mortgage payment when it comes time for renewal.

When your mortgage is written using a variable rate, or you have structured a fixed-payment strategy using a variable rate, your mortgage will most definitely be impacted. The only question is, how much? You will receive a 30-day notice from most lenders (but not all) before a base rate change will affect your payment. The annual review is important to reflect how the changes throughout the year have impacted your original plan. Does the base rate change lengthen your mortgage-free date or shorten it? How much does the change affect your total payment and the portion paid to interest? How many more increases are you comfortable with? Each aspect is an important discussion to have with your professional mortgage advisor.

Principal Reduction from Prepayment Privileges

Another part of your plan you will want to review annually at a minimum is the amount of principal reduction you have taken advantage of through prepayment privileges. If you recall the explanation of prepayment privileges from Chapter Five, there are different strategies to pay down part of the principal without interest penalties.

If your plan includes principal reduction, your annual review is the perfect time to verify your behaviors are in line with your plan. Take a moment to calculate how much interest you are going to save over the next 20-30 years because of the extra principal you paid down. Then give yourself a high five!

If your plan did not include any principal reduction, the annual review is a good time to discuss how your income situation may have changed over the past year. Perhaps you received a pay increase at work or were able to save some money on living expenses you hadn't expected. Whatever your situation, the annual review is another opportunity to ensure your mortgage is working for you and not just the lender! This is also a good opportunity to calculate the amount of interest you COULD be saving over the next 20-30 years if you DID use your prepayment privileges. Remember, even an extra $155 per month can save you many thousands of dollars.

New Posted Rates

You might be wondering why I would suggest an annual review is a good time to review the new posted rates, especially if you are only one year into a five-year term. First of all, being informed is always in your best interest. Keeping knowledgeable about all the factors which affect your financial future is your responsibility. Reviewing the latest posted rates with your professional mortgage advisor helps you stay informed about what the market has been doing and may be doing in the near future.

Second, you may be in a position to take advantage of substantial rate decreases! That's right. There is little to prevent you from exploring WIIFM for yourself. I refer to this as Opportunity Cost. A flexible mortgage structure with the right prepayment privileges may put you in a position to save a ton of interest when the new posted rates are on the decline. With the help of your professional mortgage advisor, the amount of interest savings you get from refinancing your current mortgage at a lower interest rate may offset the amount of interest penalty you would need to pay. There are many regulations surrounding these types of transactions, which is why it is so important to have your annual review with your professional mortgage advisor.

Lastly, you may observe that rates are trending upward and you may want to lock in a fixed rate (assuming you are in a variable-rate product) to prevent your payment from getting higher than you are comfortable with. This can also be done mid-term, but it requires a competent analysis from your professional mortgage advisor to review ALL the factors.

At the outset, you may feel meeting every year to review a mortgage which is scheduled for the next 20-30 years seems redundant. My wish for you is that you NOW understand the importance of the annual review and realize although your mortgage is signed and closed, that doesn't mean it should be the last time you meet with your professional mortgage advisor.

Renewals

After your 30-day follow-up and in addition to your annual reviews, another very important time for Your Big Asset is six months prior to your renewal date. The renewal date can occur several times over the course of your mortgage. The renewal happens at the end of your term (e.g. five years). Many people confuse the mortgage term with the amortization period. Recall from Chapter Eight that *the mortgage term is the length of time the rate and the term type will cover*. The term can be anywhere between six months and 10 years.

The renewal is the second most important decision you will need to make regarding your mortgage (second only to the original signing). When your mortgage comes up for renewal, your terms are likely to change. Although you may have signed a closed, five-year, fixed-rate term at 3.29% on a

$500,000 mortgage, those terms may not be available by the time it is your turn to renew. That means you are going to have to make some decisions about

- The available rates and terms.
- How will that affect your payment?
- Revisit the amortization period if needed.
- Is refinancing required?
- How does the plan need to change?

In short, this is another opportunity to revise your original plan with your professional mortgage advisor. Your life isn't going to stay the same over the next 25-30 years, so why would anyone expect your mortgage would stay the same? The economy is constantly shifting, the lenders are constantly making adjustments to maximize their profits and so should you consider all available options to protect Your Big Asset.

Six-Month Contact

The ideal time to start your renewal is six months prior to the end of your term. Why is it six months when we just had an annual review? This is the time where you will put together a new plan with your professional mortgage advisor. The process doesn't need to be long and painful. It is actually quite the opposite if you have followed all of the planning and reviews, I have suggested thus far.

The six-month contact prior to your renewal date is a great time for you and your professional mortgage advisor to catch up on any life events which may affect your plan.

Income Events	Family Events	Credit Events
Pay Increase	New Born	New debts (e.g. car loan)
Layoffs	Recent Pregnancy	Paid off debts
Inheritance	Death in the Family	Credit Difficulty
Workers Compensation	Power of Attorney	Debt Write Offs
Disability/Injury		Collections
New Job		Late Payments
Taxes		Bankruptcy
		Consumer Proposal

These are just a few of the factors that could affect your renewal and are important for your professional mortgage advisor to be aware of. These are also events which have an impact on your financial fitness. Recall the cash flow pie from Chapter One. The pie isn't fixed and is constantly shifting as your needs change. Your investment into your Big Asset isn't a sprint. It's a marathon. And it's a race you can win if you manage it properly.

Though the six-month contact serves to update your professional mortgage advisor about your current situation, it is also a chance for you to get an update about what is happening in the industry. Unless you're deeply involved on a day-to-day basis with the industry insiders, there is a good chance you may not know exactly what is going on and how it might affect you. At your six-month contact meeting, your professional mortgage advisor will be able update you on the current trends on rates and terms, what the economic forecasters may be reporting and provide you with general insight about what are the best next steps for you. Are the rates expected to go up or down in the short-term and by how much? Are the lenders' credit requirements getting tighter and how so?

> **Learning Lesson**
>
> The lender is not under any legal obligation to renew your mortgage nor are you under any obligation to renew with them. The only obligation for either party is for the term of the contract.
>
> The reasons for renewing with the same lender or choosing to sign with another lender vary with every individual. Some of the considerations should include the cost of switching lenders versus staying with the current lender, the credit worthiness of the borrower, and most importantly, financial need of the borrower.

While it is true the lender is not obligated to renew the mortgage at the end of the term, nor are you required to renew with the lender, it is not very common that a current lender will decline a renewal. That does not mean it can't or won't happen if the conditions (*5C's*) are bad enough.

The financial crisis in 2008 is one example of renewal risk. Without going into a ton of background details (that will be a different book entirely!), leading up to 2007-2008, property values were on the rise, the economy was growing steadily, while personal incomes and available cash were high. The mortgage rules were different, and homeowners could refinance up to 90% of their market value and take the equity as cash. They were like the glory days when we were living them. Not so much today.

Then the downfall began. Investors were quickly losing confidence and property values began to sink, while borrowers were losing their jobs due to mass layoffs. One of the results was many borrowers found themselves jobless and stuck in mortgages which were more than the value of the home. The term we use is that they were *underwater*, and it wasn't by just a little.

Many of these underwater mortgages were coming up for renewal and the lenders were refusing to renew them--even more so because the borrowers owed more than the property was worth and many did not have any income because of layoffs. Other lenders weren't going to refinance the mortgage for them. As if the situation wasn't serious enough, people couldn't renew their mortgages they'd been faithfully paying for several years.

The regulations throughout the mortgage industry have changed since that time and continue to evolve. The fact remains that neither the lender nor the borrower are forced to continue to renew the mortgage at the end of the contract. Hopefully by now you recognize the importance of the six-month contact prior to your renewal date. Your situation may not be as severe as it was for many people back in 2008, but this is your Big Asset. You need to take care of you. The first step is awareness.

4, 3, 2...Rate Holds

The six-month contact has a very strategic purpose for your financial plan, as there is a tactical reason. Your professional mortgage advisor will be able to work and get you the best possible terms based on your plan. You can actually hedge for the best terms possible leading up to your renewal date.

Starting four months prior to your renewal date, you can apply for an approval and rate hold. Suppose your mortgage renewal is due four months from today. A lot can change in the next four months which could cost you or save you thousands of dollars. Wouldn't it be nice if you could lock-in the best possible deal available today, but wait for a better deal to come along before your renewal?

That is exactly what the rate holds are for. Your professional advisor can submit an application to their lenders for a four-month, three-month and two-month rate hold. The process differs a little between qualifying lenders but is relatively simple. Your application goes into the lender for approval as if you are going to renew (or refinance) your mortgage for the terms at the time. Those terms can be held for 30-120 days and vary between the different lenders.

What happens if the terms are better than those for whicht you applied? Suppose the base rate goes down by 0.25% within thc next 30 days. Does that mean you are stuck? The answer is no. You can resubmit your application for the new terms and save yourself some money. Here is the hedge--if the rate goes up 0.25%, you get to keep the terms for which you've been approved, provided you close by the time they expire. You're going to get all of the upside and none of the downside.

Your professional mortgage advisor will take you through these steps at three-months and two-months prior to your renewal, which means you will close on the best possible terms available four months prior to your renewal.

This renewal process, along with rate hold periods, can be relatively simple if you are dealing only with your current lender, though there is no guarantee you are getting the best possible arrangement by settling for the default options. This is quite a big deal when even a 0.25% change can make a difference of thousands to hundreds-of-thousands of dollars. That is why working with a competent and professional mortgage advisor is in your best interest. They work for you. Imagine trying to update the rate holds across 10-20 different lenders if you attempted to shop your renewal on your own.

Do you think one 45-minute meeting six months prior to your renewal is worth it? The answer is *yes* or *yes*.

It wouldn't seem reasonable to invest $500,000 into an asset and simply say, "Okay, let me know how it does in 25-30 years." I know that doesn't REALLY happen with your Big Asset because you see it and can touch it every day. Sadly, that is how most people deal with their financial futures. They come up with a plan which appears to work at the moment and hope it's going to work out over the next 30 years. Your home isn't like a pot roast you can just put in the oven to *Set It and Forget It*.

That's why I am so excited you are reading this book. If you didn't know how often you should be in touch with your professional mortgage advisor before, you certainly know now. You now know you need to schedule a 30-day Follow-Up after closing, a review every year after you receive your mortgage statement from your lender and start the renewal process six months before your renewal date.

There is one final element. This one last piece covers all other events that we can't possibly anticipate or put on a calendar. The last piece is to contact your professional mortgage advisor whenever you need help. This relationship continues on long past the date of the transaction. As a trusted advisor, they want to be there to help you whenever you need them. Notify your adviser whenever you experience a major life event. Having a baby? Notify your advisor. Changing jobs? Notify your advisor. Thinking about renting out your extra room? Notify your advisor. Building a basement suite? Notify your advisor.

Your advisor has a ton of resources available to them. They may have some insights as to how your Big Asset can be used as leverage. They may have ideas about how your home can be used to help when times get tough or provide some direction to reduce your cost of borrowing when you find yourself with a little extra cash.

Your advisor also has industry contacts. They can put you in touch with competent and professional insurance advisors to help you protect your income and your assets. Your professional mortgage advisor also has solid contacts if you need investment advice. Thinking about renovating or need repairs? Your advisor also has contacts with general contractors and other construction specialists who can help renovate your basement, repair your roof or install siding. Landscapers, Plumbers and Realtors are all part of the team to which your advisor has access.

It takes an entire team to help you get the most value and enjoyment from your Big Asset. All you need to recognize is your professional mortgage advisor is your primary contact. Think of them first.

Ideas to Remember

- The closing of your mortgage contract is the beginning and not the end.
- You should plan to meet with your professional mortgage advisor at regular intervals over the term of your mortgage.
- The 30-day follow-up is the first meeting you should schedule with your advisor after closing to get any reminders of details you may have forgotten.
- The annual statement from your lender is your signal to schedule an annual review with your advisor.
- The renewal process actually starts six months prior to your renewal date.
- Rate holds at four-months, three-months and two-months prior to your renewal date help you take advantage of the best possible terms at your renewal.
- Any life event is worthy of sharing with your professional mortgage advisor. They have access to a ton of resources
- which can help you get the most value and enjoyment out of your BigAsset

CHAPTER TEN
HOMEOWNER FOR LIFE

"Where we love is home - home that our feet may leave,
but not our hearts."

~ Oliver Wendell Holmes, Sr.

Once you become a homeowner, you will be a homeowner for life. Either you will own the home you live in for the rest of your life or you will own several homes as part of a much bigger financial plan. Your home becomes part of your heart. There is something to be said about the saying, "Home is where the heart is." I believe that to be true. I also believe that the connection becomes 100x stronger when you own your home.

This is one of the many reasons why I became a professional mortgage advisor. It is also one of the reasons for writing this book. I love to be a part of helping great people and amazing families find that feeling of home. Another one of my favorite quotes comes from Mother Teresa:

"Love begins by taking care of the closest ones - the ones at home."

That is why I feel you will be a homeowner for life. Consider the following passage:[xxx]

What Owning a Home Means to Me

OWNING my home means saying, `I Can!'

I can provide stability for my family in an ever-changing world.

I can immediately seize control of my life.

I can say goodbye to landlords, and hello to principles of commitment, hard work and reliability. These necessary tools will keep me rooted securely in my home to demonstrate to the next generation that a perfect mixture of determination, devotion, patience and confidence are a winning solution to homeownership status.

Owning my home means giving back to the community and saying yes to the protection of our homes and the fundamental basics of a strong community. Homeowners accept responsibility for their part of the world and are committed to the continued enrichment and empowerment of that community.

Homeownership means I am not a quitter. I will take chances and explore new ideas. It says I am smart enough to achieve my dreams and I won't be afraid of the unknown. I will have enough stamina to meet the challenges and determination to face the obstacles.

Homeownership gives me liberty to express myself freely without prohibitions. I can exercise my right to embellish that little space between the commode and the bathtub with as much flair or simplicity as desired. I can paint my guest room electric purple with a lime-green border and love it! I can plant perennials in the spring and make Frosty the Snowman in the winter. Homeownership means being me!

Being a homeowner means welcoming in relaxation and snuggling up to the comfort. It means openly embracing each new perspective accompanied with that home and accepting it. It means providing a safe haven for children to play and having intentional concern for home beyond my front porch.

Homeownership means positive interaction to produce solidarity in the community.

Homeownership means gaining peace and strength for my inner soul. Believing with a certain degree of timing and ingenuity, I can achieve anything.

So ultimately, owning a home means I'm successful and able to say `Yes.' Yes, I'm a positive role model for my children! Yes, I'll take responsibility for my life! Yes, I'm worthy, dependable and self-motivated!

It also means saying `No.' No, life will not pass me by! No, I won't lose control of my future and fold to life's challenges! Instead, I will take them on, feet planted firmly and bellow out, `Mountain! Get out of my way!'

Homeownership means I refuse to give up or in and I won't bow down until I've exhausted every avenue, corner and back alley.

My motto is, `I'm in it to win!' That means no mountain is too high or river too wide to keep me from homeownership status!

Owning my home means telling myself, `I love you' and `Welcome' to the world. But most importantly, owning my home means saying, `I Can!'

This article was written by LaTasha Lee in 1999 for the Baltimore Sun. I wanted to share this with you because of the power her message holds. Home ownership means so much more than just having a place to live or an asset which appreciates. That's what it means to be a homeowner for life.

Power of the Asset

Ask not what you can do for your home. Ask what your home can do for you. I apologize. I couldn't resist my little spoof on a very famous quote by former U.S. President John F. Kennedy. After all of the validation, sense of accomplishment and feelings of belonging, your home is an asset and it has power.

Take a look at the scale above. Net worth is the difference between your Assets and Liabilities. If your assets are worth more than your liabilities, you have a positive net worth. If your assets are less than your liabilities, you have a negative net worth.

Without getting into a detailed debate about the definitions, the simplest way to look at net worth is everything you own minus everything you owe. There are many discussions about what an asset is. There is little need to discuss those here because as I have mentioned before, I like to keep things simple.

Your home is a powerful asset. It doesn't behave like most other assets.

Versus Paper Assets

Paper assets include such items as investments into stocks, bonds or certain cash-value insurance policies. These are types of assets which an investor buys with the expectation they will grow in value which creates a capital gain. The gain is realized when the investment is then sold at its market value.

You probably already know the values of these assets can decline, and sometimes very quickly. When the value gets to $0, the entire investment is gone and cannot be recovered. The principal investment is gone, and the investor takes a loss.

Your home is a powerful asset in the sense that the value rarely declines. Take a look at the historical growth rates of average housing pricing in Canada over 32 years.[xxxi]

Canada: Average prices, all home types (% growth)								
1984	1988	1992	1996	2000	2004	2008	2012	2016
$76,351	$129,702 (70%)	$149,864 (16%)	$150,899 (1%)	$164,374 (9%)	$226,604 (38%)	$304,663 (34%)	$363,606 (19%)	$442,264 (21%)

Some periods show lower growth rates than others, but none show a decline. The same cannot be said for the paper assets of stocks and bonds in the same time periods.

Versus Other Hard Assets

A *hard asset* is an investment you make in an asset you can touch and take possession of. Your home is a type of hard asset. The other hard assets to which I am referring include gold, silver, other precious metals and commodities you can buy and take possession of. This also includes investment-grade diamonds and cash accounts (deposit/savings accounts). Though many of these are also available as paper assets (e.g. futures, REIT, etc.), for this discussion, we will assume an investor will take possession of these items.

Similar to paper assets, an investor buys these assets with the expectation of a growth in value. Similarly, they can also be worth less than the principal investment used to buy them, though the respective volatility may be a little less. The biggest difference here is possession. An investor holds a hard asset. You can take possession of your diamond investment, you can put your gold into a safe, and you can hold onto your home (figuratively).

One issue present with these other hard assets is how difficult they are to sell for the everyday investor. It is actually pretty easy to buy a gold or silver coin. It is also relatively easy to buy an investment-grade diamond. But they are considerably more difficult to sell. Each hard asset requires a specific exchange, brokerage, or auction to sell these items. The sale needs to be managed by some sort of broker.

This is the power of your home as an asset. The market to sell your home is public and with a light touch from a real estate professional, is relatively simple to sell compared to other hard assets.

Versus Equipment

Machinery and equipment are also other types of assets which depreciate in value. A car is also included in this group. All these assets lose value over time. So why are they assets? Simply because they can be used to generate cash. A business can use their machinery or equipment to produce a product they can sell, and with which may generate cash. Your car can be used as service (see Uber or Lyft) to generate cash flow.

These assets continue to depreciate until they reach close to $0 or scrap value. Your home can be used to generate cash, but it DOES NOT depreciate in value. You can rent out a room (see AirBnB) or the entire home as a rental property to generate cash flow. That is the power of your Big Asset!

Over the last nine (and a bit) chapters, I wanted to share as much information and insight as I could in these pages. You are the reason for me writing this book. I care about you and your financial well-being. I need to drop a truth bomb on you right now. You are responsible for your own financial well-being and no one will care as much about your financial fitness as you.

> ***
> NO ONE WILL CARE AS MUCH ABOUT YOUR
> FINANCIAL FITNESS AS MUCH AS YOU
> ***

I care a lot about the people who choose me to help them buy their Big Asset. As I am sure when you choose a competent and professional mortgage advisor to help you, they will care equally as much about you. But none of us care quite as much about your finances as you. That's not meant to sound derogatory or offensive. I will say the same about me. There is no one in this world who will care as much about my financial well-being as me. There are many people who care a ton, like my parents or my siblings. I care just a little more about my financial fitness than they do.

This is life, and if that isn't yet your experience, then I want you to prepare yourself. There are lots of people you will need on your team to buy your Big Asset, and you need to be able to trust them. I am not suggesting you shouldn't trust them. Just *trust but verify*.

A colleague of mine shared this with me. He'd heard Dr. Nido Qubein speak at several events and one of his takeaways was *trust but verify*. This is one of the reasons I wrote this book. I want to be a part of arming you with as much information as I can, so you have enough background information to confidently evaluate the advice you are given.

In the mortgage profession, the vast majority of advisors are competent and capable. They work on your behalf with only your best interests in mind. Their job is to provide you with as much education and options as you need to make a good decision. That is their responsibility. Your responsibility is to put yourself in a position to make a good decision for yourself. No one can tell you what that is. You need to decide for yourself.

Your financial well-being is your responsibility. You have the most to gain AND the most to lose. I need you to remember this when it comes time to book your 30-day follow-up or your annual review. You may feel inconvenienced to contact your professional mortgage advisor to discuss a major life event. When you feel perhaps you can just sluff it off, remember your financial fitness is your responsibility.

The good news is you will have a ton of help. You don't need to be the expert in all things financial for you to take responsibility. I can confidently say you have an army of competent financial advisors at your fingertips to help you.

Your professional mortgage advisor has an extensive network of friends, advisors and colleagues ready to serve. Imagine having a team of 60, 70 or 100 experts available to consult with you about every aspect of your finances and not having a payroll to keep them around?!?!?!!

That's what your advisor's network is like. They have access to many types of lenders, bankers, life insurances, home and auto insurances, contractors, architects, designers, Realtors, disability insurances, title insurances, landscapers, roofers, homebuilders, and the list goes on. Your advisor also has access to home inspectors and lawyers--two very important roles in mortgaging your Big Asset.

You may not need some or all of these services today. Perhaps in six months or six years. Your advisor has a vast and diverse network they have invested thousands of hours building. All are ready to step up and help you with your Big Asset. Imagine how much time you would have to spend just to interview 10+ contractors to renovate your basement and still not be sure if they will do what they say they can do. What if you had access to a reliable contractor who has already been vetted by a trusted source? Now multiply that by the number of services you will need in over the next 10 years. That is the value your professional mortgage advisor will bring beyond just helping you purchase your home.

"I can't change the direction of the wind, but I can adjust my sails to always reach my destination."

-Jimmy Dean

There are few guarantees in life, but the fact that conditions will eventually change is one of them. The world is going to change with or without you. The question is, how are you positioned to handle the change that's coming?

Brett Roessel

1989	Berlin wall tumbled
1990	Nelson Mandela is freed
	World Wide Web is invented
1997	Princess Diana dies tragically
1998	Y2K Scare breaks news as possibility
2000	Dot Com bubble bursts
	Y2K Bug fails to happen
2001	World Trade Center attacked
2003	Space shuttle challenger explodes
2004	Massachussets 1st state to legalize same-sex marriage
2005	Hurricane Katrina
2007	Worst global financial crisis since the great depression
2008	Barack Obama elected as 1st Black U.S. President
2012	Washington and Denver legalize Marijuana
2013	Uber and AirBnB are launched
2016	Brexit Referendum
2017	Bitcoin peaks at $19,783
2018	Prince Harry gets married to Meghan Markle #MeToo Movement goes global Sears and Toys-R-Us declare bankruptcy

Some of these world events may have had an impact in your life. A few may have had a bigger impact than others. It would be difficult to find many people in the industrialized world who were not affected by the financial crisis in 2007-2008. There were many people who lost their jobs, had a drop in the value of their investments or saw their home values decline. Many people were affected by the World Trade Center attacks. The launch of Uber and AirBnB have changed the way people use their assets to generate cash flow AND how we use rideshare or accommodations in the new sharing economy.

You can probably think of hundreds of events you cannot control which have had an impact on your financial well-being and in your life. The point is this - although you cannot control the events in the world or their impact on your life, you can control how you react, adjust, or adapt to everything happening around you.

It starts early-on with your plan. You remember the one I have mentioned throughout this book? The plan you put together with your professional mortgage advisor is one of the first steps to purchasing your Big Asset, including your goals and objectives (personal and financial), the flexibility and features (prepayment privileges, fixed payments, open terms, etc.) you need today plus anticipating any you may need going forward.

Having the plan is only partly useful. The plan must be executed. The second part of this entire message is to ensure you are continuously reviewing and adjusting your plan with your professional mortgage advisor. Your plan is a living strategy which adjusts with ALL the life events you experience, many of which are not under your control, while some are yours by design.

The world is going to change with or without you. The financial responsibility is yours to maximize on your opportunities when your life is going well and according to (or better than) your plan. It is also your responsibility to minimize any damage when you are forced to deal with many of life's pitfalls when they come your way.

Take Care of Your Reputation

Credit is your reputation on paper. It is your *financial reputation for life*. I think it is important to revisit the quote, *"We are what we repeatedly do."* This quote is often mis-attributed to Aristotle and is actually credited to Will Durant, an American author born in the 1800's. Durant's statement unofficially sums up the entire credit industry and how it behaves.

The entire quote is, *"We are what we repeatedly do. Excellence, then, is not an act, but a habit."* Think about what a reputation is, or how you know when someone is trustworthy. It is because they have a good reputation for what you want them to do and have been trustworthy in the past.

This system works when you know someone well. We all have friends or family members whom we feel are very trustworthy and are bound by their word. We also know people to whom we wouldn't lend $100 because they can't be trusted to pay it back. The reason is that people generally follow their habits. If they have a habit of being trustworthy and delivering on their promises, we can expect that is their habit and they will likely continue to do so. In the same respect, those who consistently fail to deliver on their promises, no matter how big or small, are likely to continue those habits, as well.

Credit, then, is a record of your financial habits. It is your reputation of what you repeatedly do. Your credit is documentation of how you keep your financial promises and how well you keep your payment promises with creditors. If your payments are consistently up-to-date and you are what you repeatedly do, then you have a good financial reputation. The opposite is also true. A poor payment history and a string of bad debts results in a poor reputation.

How easy is it to repair a reputation of bad habits or behaviors? In other words, how easy is it for you to begin to trust someone after they have lied, cheated, stolen, or broken their promises? It is not easy. It takes a long time to rebuild a bad reputation and a short time to ruin a good one. Is it possible to change a habit? Of course, it is. But it takes time. Changing a personal habit takes time. So does changing a spending habit. Those changes, over time, will make an improvement in your reputation if something happened to go sideways. I think it's clear that we are impacted by events out of our control. What we repeatedly do IS in our control. It's not what happens to us that is measured, it's how we react that is recorded. Job loss happens. Divorces happen. Family deaths happen. Economic crises happen. We have no control over any of them. We *do* have control over how we act afterward.

Your financial fitness is your responsibility. Credit is your reputation on paper. There is too much at stake to take it lightly when it comes to the biggest purchase you are likely to make in your lifetime. Follow your plan, adjust it when necessary, meet with your professional mortgage advisor regularly and update them when important life events happen. These are all tactics to protect your reputation. When life happens, it's your team of advisors who help you protect your reputation. They know your goals and objectives and have helped you with your plan. Your team of advisors are there to help you navigate all the options open to you to help get you through times of trouble. They will help keep a negative financial experience as a small blemish in your reputation instead of a major blowout.

It takes a long time to build a strong reputation and a short time to ruin it. You are a homeowner for life and your financial well-being is up to you. Make it happen!

Ideas to Remember

- You are a homeowner for life.
- Your home is one of the most powerful assets you can own.
- Housing prices rarely decline, unlike paper assets.
- Real estate may be used to generate cash flow while not depreciating like machinery or equipment.
- Your financial well-being is your responsibility.
- Trust but verify.
- Your professional mortgage advisor has a network. Use it.
- So much that happens in life is out of your control. What you do as a result is in your control.
- Credit is your financial reputation for life.
- It takes a long time to build a good reputation and a short time to ruin it.
- Make it happen!

---

[i] FINRA Investor Education Foundation. (2015). U.S. Survey Data at a Glance. Retrieved June 1, 2018, from http://www.usfinancialcapability.org/results.php?region=US

[ii] Mccarthy, S. (2018, May 16). Many Canadians entering retirement with inadequate savings, study says. Retrieved June 1, 2018, from https://www.theglobeandmail.com/globe-investor/retirement/retire-plannin g/many-canadians-entering-retirement-with-inadequate-savings-study-says /article28761394/

[iii] Fordham. (n.d.). Ancient History Sourcebook: A Collection of Contracts from Mesopotamia, c. 2300 - 428 BCE. Retrieved June 1, 2018, from https://sourcebooks.fordham.edu/ancient/mesopotamia-contracts.asp

[iv] Chepkemoi, J. (2017, February 16). Countries with the Highest Home Ownership Rates. Retrieved June 10, 2018, from https://www.worldatlas.com/articles/countries-with-the-highest-home-own ership-rates.html

[v] Maslow's Hierarchy of Needs. (2018, May 21). Retrieved June 6, 2018, from https://www.simplypsychology.org/maslow.html

[vi] CREA. (2018, June 18). Retrieved June 1, 2018, from http://creastats.crea.ca/natl/index.html

[vii] Habitat for Humanity. (2017, November 07). Surprising Statistics on Habitat for Humanity Homeowners in Georgia. Retrieved June 1, 2018, from https://www.athenshabitat.com/homeowner-statistics-2016/

[viii] Bank of Canada. (n.d.). Historical Data. Retrieved June 1, 2018, from https://www.bankofcanada.ca/rates/indicators/capacity-and-inflation-press ures/real-estate-market-definitions/real-estate-market-historical-data/

[ix] StatsCan. (2016, September 15). Homeownership and Shelter Costs in Canada. Retrieved June 1, 2018, from http://www12.statcan.gc.ca/nhs-enm/2011/as-sa/99-014-x/99-014-x20110 02-eng.cfm

[x] Statista. (2018). Home maintenance costs by type U.S. 2017 | Statistic. Retrieved June 1, 2018, from https://www.statista.com/statistics/748004/average-monthly-maintenance-

costs-for-homes-usa/
[xi] Seabury, C. (2018, May 24). Property Taxes: How They Are Calculated. Retrieved June 1, 2018, from https://www.investopedia.com/articles/tax/09/calculate-property-tax.asp
[xii] Bula 1, F. (2017, November 12). High rent and low vacancy are squeezing renters in Canada's largest cities. Retrieved June 1, 2018, from https://www.theglobeandmail.com/news/british-columbia/rent-series-part1/article30832544/
[xiii] Genworth Canada. (n.d.). New to Canada Program. Retrieved June 1, 2018, from http://genworth.ca/en/products/new-to-canada-program.aspx
[xiv] Canada Revenue Agency. (2018, January 03). How to participate in the Home Buyers' Plan (HBP). Retrieved June 1, 2018, from https://www.canada.ca/en/revenue-agency/services/tax/individuals/topics/rsps-related-plans/what-home-buyers-plan/participate-home-buyers-plan.html#RRSP-withdrawalconditions
[xv] Warden, P. (2018, February 16). What mortgage rate history can tell us about the future. Retrieved June 1, 2018, from https://themortgagereports.com/35593/what-mortgage-rate-history-can-tell-us-about-the-future
[xvi] Hur, J. (2017, November 17). History of the 30 Year Mortgage – From Historic Rates to Present Time. Retrieved June 4, 2018, from https://bebusinessed.com/history/history-of-mortgages/
[xvii] P.P. (2018, February 28). A History of Mortgage Rule Changes in Canada. Retrieved June 2, 2018, from http://peterpaley.com/general/history-mortgage-rule-changes-canada/
[xviii] Canada New Housing Price Index | 1981-2018 | Data | Chart | Calendar. (2018). Retrieved June 5, 2018, from https://tradingeconomics.com/canada/housing-index
[xix] Statistics Canada. (2017, October 27). Housing in Canada: Key results from the 2016 Census. Retrieved June 5, 2018, from https://www150.statcan.gc.ca/n1/daily-quotidien/171025/dq171025c-eng.htm
[xx] Rivera, M. (2017, November 29). THE SILENT KILLER OF RELATIONSHIPS IS NOT UNMET EXPECTATIONS. Retrieved June

6, 2018, from https://projectmanbeyond.com/expectations/
^{xxi} *Verico Title Insurance Presentation Spring 2018*[PPTX]. (2012, October 4). Calgary: FCT.
^{xxii} Rivero, J. (2011, October 29). From Credit Scores to "Behavioral Scores": What Numbers Say About You. Retrieved June 6, 2018, from https://www.forbes.com/sites/moneywisewomen/2011/10/28/from-credit-s cores-to-behavioral-scores-what-numbers-say-about-you/#322468722073
^{xxiii} Rising Interest Rates – thanks to QE? (2010, December 16). Retrieved June 6, 2018, from https://takloo.wordpress.com/tag/historical-rates/
^{xxiv} Fixed vs Variable Mortgage Rates | Comparing Pros & Cons. (2018). Retrieved June 6, 2018, from https://www.ratehub.ca/variable-or-fixed-mortgage
^{xxv} Ratehub. (2018). Mortgage Term vs. Amortization | Loan Payment Timeline. Retrieved June 6, 2018, from https://www.ratehub.ca/mortgage-term-vs-amortization
^{xxvi} Trading Economics. (2018). Canada Household Saving Rate | 1981-2018 | Data | Chart | Calendar. Retrieved July 14, 2018, from https://tradingeconomics.com/canada/personal-savings
^{xxvii} Vanier Institute for the Family. (2018, January). Modern Family Finances: Income in Canada (January 2018). Retrieved July 15, 2018, from http://vanierinstitute.ca/modern-family-finances-income-canada-january-2 018/
^{xxviii} CIBC. (2017, November 21). Why is it so hard to save? Most Canadians say they 'need to save more,' but aren't making it a priority: CIBC Poll. Retrieved July 15, 2018, from https://www.newswire.ca/news-releases/why-is-it-so-hard-to-save-most-ca nadians-say-they-need-to-save-more-but-arent-making-it-a-priority-cibc-p oll-659017433.html
^{xxix} Canada Revenue Agency. (2018, January 03). How to participate in the Home Buyers' Plan (HBP). Retrieved July 15, 2018, from https://www.canada.ca/en/revenue-agency/services/tax/individuals/topics/r rsps-related-plans/what-home-buyers-plan/participate-home-buyers-plan.h tml#qualifyinghome

[xxx] Lee, L. (1999, December 26). 'What owning a home means to me'. Retrieved July 20, 2018, from http://articles.baltimoresun.com/1999-12-26/business/9912230012_1_hom e-means-homeownership-owning-a-home

[xxxi] https://www.crea.ca/